THE POWER OF
DAILY MASS

"This book is not just for those who don't yet go to daily Mass, but also for those who do. It reveals how powerful and relevant each Mass is for our lives, and will inspire and challenge you to really make the Eucharist your 'daily bread.'"

Vinny Flynn
Author of *7 Secrets of the Eucharist*

"Bert Ghezzi invites us to celebrate the blessings of daily Mass. He shows how the various parts of the Mass, culminating in the reception of the Eucharist, contain a rainbow of reasons why daily Mass is so valuable. Ample use of quotations from Church fathers, theologians, saints, and daily Mass attendees add vibrancy to his words. I highly recommend this book to Catholics looking for a guide to live a holy life."

Rev. Robert J. Hater
Author of *Common Sense Catechetics*

"Bert Ghezzi does a masterful job of telling Catholics about *The Power of Daily Mass*. He is thorough, helping readers to remember the power of the Eucharist and the need to take time after Mass to contemplate the goodness of God. This book will help anyone who wants to understand both the Mass and the Catholic Church. Don't overlook the appendices."

Deacon Henry Libersat
Author of *Catholic and Confident*

How Frequent

Participation

in the Eucharist Can

Transform Your Life

THE POWER OF
DAILY MASS

BERT GHEZZI

ave maria press AMP notre dame, indiana

Founded in 1865, Ave Maria Press is a ministry of the United States Province of Holy Cross.

www.avemariapress.com

Paperback: ISBN-13 978-1-59471-562-4

E-book: ISBN-13 978-1-59471-563-1

Cover image © Agnus Images.

Cover and text design by Katherine Robinson.

Printed and bound in the United States of America.

Library of Congress Cataloging-in-Publication Data

Ghezzi, Bert.

   The power of daily mass : how frequent participation in the Eucharist can transform your spiritual life / Bert Ghezzi.

      pages cm

Includes bibliographical references and index.

ISBN 978-1-59471-562-4 -- ISBN 1-59471-562-9

   1. Lord's Supper--Frequency of communion 2. Mass--Frequency of celebration. 3. Lord's Supper--Catholic Church. I. Title.

BX2236.6.G44 2015

   264'.36--dc23

                          2014037306

For the Daily Mass Community

at

St. Mary Magdalen Catholic Church,

Altamonte Springs, Florida

Also by Bert Ghezzi

The Heart of Catholicism
Voices of the Saints
The Saints Devotional Bible (compiler / editor)
Prayers to the Holy Spirit
Discover Christ (coauthor)
Saints at Heart
Everyday Encounters with God (coauthor)
The Sign of the Cross
Mystics and Miracles
Living the Sacraments
Getting Free

Contents

Preface

For the past eight years, I have attended daily Mass at my parish. I gather at 7 a.m. with a community of men and women who have become my close friends. When I decided to write this book, I asked many of them to tell me about the effect daily Mass has had on their lives. They reported a variety of benefits:

Daily Mass . . .

- gives me courage and hope to face daily challenges and problems;
- lets me participate in the greatest of miracles—the Eucharistic presence of our Lord and Savior, Jesus Christ;
- makes me aware of how much God loves me;
- realigns me to God's plan for my life;
- allows me to feel free to talk to the Lord;
- gives me an opportunity to intercede for family and friends.

You will read more of their observations in the following pages. Once I asked a young visitor to our 7 a.m. liturgy why he came to Mass. He said, "Because I love Jesus." His heartfelt response undergirds all the other beneficial effects my friends reported.

I experience many of the same benefits. I especially take away from the readings a word that encourages me or gives me direction. Today, for example, I heard the Lord speak to me about calming my irritability with these words from James: "Be . . . slow to anger, for anger does not accomplish the righteousness of God" (Jas 1:19–20). I need to do that because I don't want to be a hearer only.

The highlight for me is receiving the Lord's Body and Blood in Communion. That the God who fashioned the universe of 300 billion trillion stars comes to me fills me with awe. As I kneel in reflection, I often remember Curtis Martin's profound observation that we are "living monstrances," bearing the Real Presence into our lives and relationships.[1]

Worshiping at daily Mass offers you all these benefits and more. I designed this little book to describe them and show how to receive them. Each chapter presents one aspect of our participation in the Lord's eternal sacrifice, and each chapter gives you a chance to reflect on the graces we receive as we celebrate the re-presentation of the death and resurrection of Jesus. As you read this book, you will review with me the way daily Mass forgives little sins; allows you to hear God speaking to you in scripture; gives you the opportunity both to offer yourself to God and also to offer Christ's sacrifice with him; provides spiritual nourishment from eating Christ's Body and drinking his Blood; and strengthens you for your day's activities and challenges.

The Power of Daily Mass is a book for all Catholics. Those who already attend daily Mass will it inspires them by broadening their understanding and reinforcing their experience. It will encourage those who attend once in a while to get to daily Mass more regularly, and I hope the book will persuade many others to consider building Mass into their daily routine.

Acknowledgments

The faithful commitment of my sisters and brothers at my parish's daily Mass community convinced me to write this book and they greatly influenced its content. Thanks to all of you. Thanks, too, to my friend George Martin, whose suggestions made this a better book. I am also grateful to Robert Hamma, the editorial director of Ave Maria Press, who asked me to write *The Power of Daily Mass*. I resisted the idea at first, thinking that I might be able to write an article on the topic rather than a book, but he persisted and persuaded me to write the book, and I'm glad that he did. I am indebted to the whole staff at Ave Maria Press for their very competent service to me.

Chapter 1

Every Day **with Jesus**

> I have grown in my understanding that
> what Jesus said and did all those many
> years ago is now present in real time. We are
> in real time sitting with Jesus at the Lord's
> Supper, standing at the foot of the cross,
> with Mary Magdalen at the empty tomb,
> with the disciples behind locked doors.
> —Henry L., a daily Mass attendee

The Church invites us to worship at Mass every day, and it
assures us that we will receive the power of daily Mass. It
does this by making the mysteries of Christ and his graces
present and available to us through the seasons of the liturgical year.

The Liturgical Year

We organize our lives according to overlapping calendars.
We follow the annual seasons from spring to winter. We
mark our time with work and school schedules. We have
fiscal calendars that tell us when our bills are due. Annu-
ally, we celebrate holidays that commemorate people and

events: Presidents' Day, Memorial Day, Independence Day, Veterans Day, and so on. We have personal calendars that track important occasions in our life. For example, for the past decade my brother-in-law has compiled the annual "Ghezzi Family Calendar." I consult it frequently to remember to greet my sixteen grandchildren on their birthdays.

As Christians, we live by a different sort of calendar called the liturgical year. As it progresses, the liturgical year brings us into a daily relationship with Jesus. "Within the cycle of a year," said the bishops at the Second Vatican Council, the Church "unfolds the whole mystery of Christ, from the incarnation and birth until the ascension, the day of Pentecost, and the expectation of blessed hope and of the coming of the Lord."[1]

These events represented in the liturgical year are not locked in the past like historical events. For example, we can only celebrate the signing of the Declaration of Independence with books, movies, blog posts, reenactments, parades, and fireworks. We can imagine looking over the shoulders of Thomas Jefferson as he wrote it, but we cannot get back to the event to re-present it.

During the course of the liturgical year, the Church actually brings us into the presence of Christ in the saving events of his life. "Recalling thus the mysteries of redemption," said the bishops at Vatican II, "the Church opens to the faithful the riches of her Lord's powers and merits, so that these are in some way made present for all time, and the faithful are enabled to lay hold upon them and become filled with saving grace."[2]

For example, forty days after Easter we celebrate Christ's ascension to his Father in heaven, but we don't remember it merely as a past event. By grace, the Lord's ascension is present to us and we rise to heaven with Christ because we are in him. St. Augustine explains this in a sermon on the feast:

Today our Lord Jesus Christ ascended into heaven; let our hearts ascend with him. Listen to the words of the Apostle: *If you have risen with Christ, set your hearts on things that are above where Christ is, seated at the right hand of God; seek the things that are above, not the things that are on earth* (Col 3:1–2). For just as he remained with us after his ascension, so we too are already in heaven with him, even though what is promised us has not yet been fulfilled in our bodies. . . . Out of compassion for us he descended from heaven, and although he ascended alone, we also ascend because we are in him by grace.[3]

Never Boring, Always Sacred, Very Practical

As we live and celebrate each liturgical year (and each year is different), we are reminded:

- life is far from ordinary, boring routine;
- every moment of time is sacred;
- the whole of salvation history . . . is gradually unpacked and pondered over in the year's seasons and feasts, keeping the paschal mystery at the heart of our lives;
- celebrating these sacred events helps us to adopt Jesus' lifestyle here and now.[4]

—Janet Schaeffler, O.P.

Thus, the liturgical year brings us immeasurable benefits. Celebrating its seasons at Sunday Mass and daily Mass opens us afresh to the riches of Christ's mercy and resets our hearts on the mystery of his death and resurrection. Our daily worship unites us with the Lord, who gives us the grace we need to pattern our lives on his teaching and example.

"Arriving early for Mass allows me to get an hour with God."

—Geraldine G.

Celebrating the Liturgical Seasons

The liturgical year takes us though five seasons—Advent, Christmas, Lent, Easter, and Ordinary Time. "In the Liturgical Year," says the *US Catechism for Adults*, "the Church celebrates the whole mystery of Christ from the Incarnation until the day of Pentecost and the expectation of Christ's second coming. . . . The presence of the Risen Lord and his saving work permeates the entire Liturgical Year: Advent, the Christmas Season, Lent, the Easter Season, and Ordinary Time."[5] The Sunday liturgies announce the themes for each season and the daily Masses develop them and apply them to our lives.

Advent

The liturgical year begins with Advent, which is marked by four consecutive Sundays from the one nearest to November 30 to the one before Christmas Day. The season prepares our hearts to welcome three comings of Jesus. Both the Christian and secular traditions focus us on Christ's first coming among us at Christmas. The season also anticipates his second coming at the end of time. Finally, woven through the Sunday and weekday liturgies of Advent is the Lord's coming to make his home in each of us (see Jn 14:23). It is a joyful time of prayer and of making room for Christ in our lives.

A Season of Devout and Expectant Delight

Advent has a twofold character, for it is a time of preparation for the Solemnities of Christmas, in which the First Coming of the Son of God to humanity is remembered, and likewise a time, when by remembrance of this, minds and hearts are led to look forward to Christ's Second Coming at the end of time. For these two reasons, Advent is a period of devout and expectant delight.[6]

—"Universal Norms on the Liturgical Year and the Calendar"

Christmas Season

This season extends from Christmas Day until the Sunday after the Epiphany. On the feast of the Nativity, we celebrate Jesus' first coming, the startling reality that God came among us as a baby. Pope Benedict XVI said that "God made himself small so that we could understand him, welcome him, and love him." We may be surprised that during Christmas time we acknowledge Jesus' Second Coming as king of all to wrap up history at the end of time. The season climaxes with the Epiphany, remembering the visit of the Magi to the baby king, which represents his coming for all humankind.

God Comes as a Baby

God makes himself small for us. This is how he reigns. He does not come with power and outward splendor. He comes as a baby—defenseless and in need of our help. He does not want to overwhelm us with his strength. He takes away our fear of his greatness. He asks for our love: so he makes himself a child. God made himself small so that we could understand him, welcome him, and love him. Let us allow our heart, our soul, and our mind to be touched by this fact.[7]

—Pope Benedict XVI

"The greatest benefit of daily Mass has been the closeness I've felt to the Lord. It's difficult to drift away from him, spiritually or morally, when you unite with him each morning, body to body, soul to soul. Daily Mass has become an anchor in my life that keeps me from sailing off to a 'distant country' (see Lk 15:13)."

—Brandon V.

Lent

Lent runs from Ash Wednesday until the Mass of the Lord's Supper on Holy Thursday. "Lent" derives from a Germanic word that means "spring." As at root, the word "Lent" indicates a time of new life; it stands as an appropriate name for this season that prepares candidates for the new life of baptism at the Easter Vigil. It calls all Christians to repentance in preparation for renewing their life in Christ at Easter.

Many Catholics celebrate this penitential season by rearranging their schedule so they can worship at daily Mass. During the first three weeks, the daily liturgies instruct us in the ways of repentance—prayer, fasting, and almsgiving (see Mt 1–6, 16–18)—and lead us to reform our lives. The Masses of the second three weeks, which reach a peak in Holy Week, immerse us daily in the events leading to the passion and death of the Lord. These days draw us to Jesus and infuse us with love and devotion for him.

Turning Lenten Penance Outward

Right at the beginning of Lent, on the Friday after Ash Wednesday, the liturgy turns our inward penance outward to works of mercy with this reading:

> Is this not . . . the fast that I choose:
> releasing those bound unjustly,
> untying the thongs of the yoke;
> Setting free the oppressed,
> breaking off every yoke?
> Is it not sharing your bread with the hungry,
> bringing the afflicted and the homeless into your house;

Clothing the naked when you see them,
and not turning your back on your own flesh?
Then your light shall break forth like the dawn. . . .
and your wound shall quickly be healed;
Your vindication shall go before you,
and the glory of the Lord shall be your rear guard.

—Isaiah 58:6-8

Easter

Lent culminates in Easter. Easter begins with the Sacred Triduum, which is Latin for "three days." It refers to the three most important days of the liturgical year: Holy Thursday, Good Friday, and Holy Saturday, which climaxes in the celebration of the Lord's resurrection at the Easter Vigil. "Christ redeemed us all," says the *Ceremonial of Bishops*, "and gave perfect glory to God principally through his paschal mystery: dying he destroyed our death, rising he restored our life. Therefore, the Easter Triduum of the Passion and Resurrection of the Lord is the culmination of the entire liturgical year."[8] If you are only able to attend daily Mass occasionally, you cannot afford to miss participating in the liturgies of these three special days.

Easter time extends for fifty days, from Easter Sunday until Pentecost. The famous line from St. Augustine—"We are an Easter people and Alleluia is our song"—expresses the joyful spirit of the season's daily Masses.

Endless Easter

Christ the Victor over death,
Breathes on us the Spirit's breath!
Paradise is our reward,
Endless Easter with our Lord.[9]

Ordinary Time

Ordinary Time occurs in two periods. The first part of the season runs between the Epiphany and Ash Wednesday. It picks up again on the Monday after Pentecost and continues until the First Sunday of Advent. On Sundays, this season draws us into the fullness of the mystery of Christ, and the daily Masses foster our growth in the Christian life. They lead us to repentance, surrender to God, and the experience of his love.

"I go primarily because I want to **worship Jesus** in the way he established as the summit of our faith. Liturgical worship in the Mass is the primary way that I can **respond to God with thanksgiving and gratitude** for his

immeasurable, magnanimous gift of
redemption and reconciliation."
—Mike M.

As you reflect on this running summary of the liturgical seasons, I hope you will decide to worship at daily Mass. If you can't make it every day, choose one or two days that fit your schedule. I assure you that you will experience the power of daily Mass. As the *Ceremonial of Bishops* says, "The celebration of the liturgical year possesses a distinct sacramental force and efficacy because Christ himself in his mysteries . . . continues his mission of infinite mercy. Therefore his faithful people not only recall and contemplate the mysteries of redemption, but also lay hold of them, enter into communion with them, and live by them."[10]

Comprehension and Discussion Questions

1. How do the events remembered in the liturgical year differ from other historical events?

2. How does the liturgical year bring us into a daily relationship with Jesus?

3. What three comings of Christ do we celebrate in Advent?

4. Why does Pope Benedict XVI say Christ made himself small to come to us?

5. What is the Sacred Triduum? Why does the Church describe it as the summit of the liturgical year?

Chapter 2

Honoring the Saints

Raised up to perfection by the manifold grace of God, and already in possession of eternal salvation, [the saints] sing God's perfect praise in heaven and offer prayers for us. By celebrating the passage of these saints from earth to heaven the Church proclaims the paschal mystery achieved in the saints who have suffered and been glorified with Christ; she proposes them to the faithful as examples drawing all to the Father through Christ, and through their merits she pleads for God's favors.[1]

—Second Vatican Council

We often celebrate birthdays at daily Mass—the birthdays of the saints. We remember not their births on earth, but their births into heaven. Every year on occasional days the Church takes us through the Cycle of Saints, from the commemoration of Mary, the Mother of God on January 1 to that of Pope St. Sylvester I on December 31.[2] Of the thousands of saints recognized by the Church, the Cycle features only those of universal significance and reserves the remembrance of others to their country, region, or religious community.

I take great pleasure celebrating the birthdays of saint-friends like St. Teresa of Avila and St. Francis of Assisi. I'm delighted to honor saints I first met at Mass, like St. Fidelis of Sigmaringen and St. Peter Chanel, both martyred for their faith. I had to do some research on Fidelis and Peter. You will need to do the same when you encounter saints at Mass that are new to you.

Holiness for All

Too often we have put the saints on pedestals, imagining that their degree of holiness is beyond our reach, but the saints we meet at daily Mass are ordinary women and men just like you and me. They have not fallen perfect from heaven nor do they have some superhuman DNA. Like us, the saints were good, but, also like us, they faced big challenges. Some were overworked and financially strapped; some were crippled with doubts, fears, and scruples; some were betrayed by friends or slandered by enemies; some were entrapped in sin and had to find the grace to fight their way to freedom, and so on.

The Splendid and Possible Standard

The abiding temptation of every Christian is to feel that the standard set by Christ is high and holy, but quite simply beyond our powers; it is splendid but impossible. The feeling is foolish, of course. The God who made men would not know so little of the beings he made as to ask the impossible of them. But knowing it is foolish does not diminish its force. We feel that however it may be for others, our peculiar circumstances and difficulties make the living of Christ's life impossible for us.

Here is a special value of the saints. Men and women of our own sort, in our circumstances, beset by our difficulties, have attained high and heroic sanctity. As this comes home to us, holiness will still seem difficult, but it will no longer seem impossible. And between the difficult and the impossible there is all the difference in the world.[3]

—F. J. Sheed

The saints we celebrate at daily Mass challenge us to imitate their holiness, but what must we do to become a saint? St. Thomas Aquinas's sister asked him that question, and he said, "Will it!" He did not mean that sheer will-power would make us saints—it doesn't have the strength to do it. Rather, Thomas taught that once we choose to become a saint, God puts us on the path to holiness and gives us a stream of graces to get us there. On saints' feast days I like to renew my decision to be a saint and I invite you to do the same.

Once we have decided to be holy, the Church holds up the saints as examples, intercessors, and companions. Honoring different saints at daily Mass illustrates these ways that they help us.

"Daily Mass gives me an opportunity to include prayers to special saints that I talk to throughout the day, such as St.

Joseph, St. Jude, and St. Anthony. I have

great faith in many of
the saints, especially St. Joseph."

—Helen S.

Giving Good Example

The Church recognizes some men and women as saints so that we may imitate their lives—not that we should become just like them, for we are unique individuals and the Lord wants us to be holy in our own way. We should become avid saint-watchers, exploring their good example for clues to better Christian living. "You should go round from saint to saint," said St. Philip Neri, "imploring an alms with the same real earnestness with which the poor beg."[4]

I have learned many things from the saints, and on their feast days I renew my application of their lessons. St. Teresa of Avila, the great pray-er and reformer, taught me that I must keep prayer and action in balance. I learned the fundamental value of integrity from St. Thomas More, who gave his life rather than betray the faith. I now strive to do little things with love, having observed the humble service of St. Thérèse of Lisieux. The example of St. Francis of Assisi, who brought so many people to Christ and the Church, fires my zeal for evangelization. St. John Bosco, the celebrated educator of homeless boys, showed me how to discipline my family with love and to serve the poor more generously. I could go on, but you get the point.

I encourage you to keep track of lessons the saints have taught you and to reflect on what you have learned on their feast days.

Interceding for Us

Being more closely united to Christ, those who dwell in heaven fix the whole Church more firmly in holiness. . . . They do not cease to intercede with the Father for us, as they proffer the merits which they acquired on earth through the one mediator between God and men, Christ Jesus. . . . So by their fraternal concern is our weakness greatly helped.

—*Catechism of the Catholic Church*, 956

The Church gives us the saints as intercessors and expects us to ask them to pray for our concerns. Invoking the saints is a longstanding practice among Catholics, who pray novenas, litanies, and special devotions. The intercession of the saints is also imbedded in the liturgies of their feasts. For example, I randomly opened the *Roman Missal* to the memorial of Pope St. Sylvester I and found this prayer:

> Come, O Lord, to the help of your people, sustained by the intercession of Pope Saint Sylvester, so that, running the course of this present life under your guidance, we may happily attain life without end. Though our Lord Jesus Christ, your Son, who lives and reigns with you in the unity of the Holy Spirit, one God for ever and ever.[5]

The saints themselves expected to be doing the work of intercession once they got to heaven. St. Dominic assured his friars that he could accomplish more for them after his death than he could in life. On the way to his execution, St. Thomas More stopped to assure a man he had always prayed for that death would not stop his interceding for him. St. Thérèse of Lisieux promised to respond to requests by asking God to flood the world with little miracles, and thousands testify that she has kept her word. The saint we turn to most often for intercession is the Queen of All Saints, Mary, who was influential enough with her Son at Cana to get him to adjust the timing of God's plan (see Jn 2:4).

You may have noticed, as I have, that some form of suffering afflicted all the saints. They experienced serious illness, opposition, failure, unfaithful spouses, rebellious children, corrupt leaders, and more. When we are suffering in similar ways, we can especially count on the saints to intercede for us. "When we undergo similar difficulties," says saint-watcher James Martin, S.J., "it's consoling to know not only there were Christians who underwent such trials, but also that, united with God, the saints are able to pray for us as we suffer. . . . Like an experienced traveler a saint can guide you along the path of suffering."[6]

"For me, daily Mass is an exchange. I bring my jumbled life to God—the problems, the concerns—and I give it to God during the Mass. He takes it and figures it out for me, often laying the answer at my feet. In the meantime, I receive him so I can go out and carry him into the world."

—Debbie T.

Companions along the Way

Celebrating the festivals of Mary and the saints remind us that the Lord has given them to us as companions who protect and guide us. The *Catechism* says that the saints who join us for worship in the liturgy stay with us to encourage us in our Christian lives: "By keeping the memorials of the saints—first of all the holy Mother of God, then the apostles, the martyrs, and other saints—on fixed days of the liturgical year, the Church on earth shows that she is united with the liturgy of heaven. She gives glory to Christ for having accomplished his salvation in his glorified members; their example encourages her on her way to the Father" (*Catechism of the Catholic Church*, 1195).

The Desires of Our Heart

Calling the saints to mind inspires, or rather arouses in us above all else, a longing to enjoy their company, so desirable in itself. We long to share in the citizenship of heaven, to dwell with the spirits of the blessed, to join the assembly of patriarchs, the ranks of the prophets, the council of apostles, the great host of martyrs, the noble company of confessors and the choir of virgins. In short, we long to be united in happiness with all the saints.

When we commemorate the saints we are inflamed with another yearning; that Christ our life may also appear to us as he appeared to them and that we may one day share in his glory.[7]

—St. Bernard of Clairvaux

We are involved personally with men and women who now live with God in heaven. From the earliest days, Christians have spoken about this "communion of saints," as we still do when we pray the Apostles' Creed. We earthly saints are linked with a vast community of heavenly saints, who accompany us and give us their support.

Mary and the saints invite us to decide to become saints, show us how to do it, pray for our success, and help us along the way—especially on their feast days.

For Comprehension and Discussion

1. What is the Cycle of Saints? Which saints are included in it?

2. In what ways are the saints like us?

3. Why does F. J. Sheed say that it's not true that sanctity is "splendid but impossible"?

4. What does St. Thomas Aquinas say a person must do to become a saint? How can that happen?

5. Which of the three reasons the Church gives us saints (exemplars, intercessors, companions) do you regard as most important for your life? Why?

Chapter 3

Daily **Repentance**

Daily Mass assures me that I have been forgiven of my sins. It helps me think more about the feelings and needs of others. I am now able to deal with my desire to judge others. I try never to do that.

—Paul M.

Our Daily Little Sins

Every day we pile up little sins. Some are faults that just slip out of us almost unnoticed. We thoughtlessly embroider the truth, idly entertain a bad thought, carelessly spurt out an inconsiderate remark, and so on. Sometimes we are aware of these little sins and just tolerate our bad behavior. When we spill a glass of milk or someone cuts us off in traffic, we blurt out an angry expletive and chalk it up to our being irritable by nature.

The Church calls these slips, whether deliberate or not, "venial" sins. The word *venial* comes from a Latin root that means "pardonable" or "excusable." The Church's use of the term suggests that grace is readily available to remit our little sins.

19

Unlike serious, or "mortal," sin, venial sin does not destroy our union with the Lord, but little faults do chip away at our divine relationship. As we accumulate venial sins, they incline us on a slippery slope to serious wrong-doing. St. Augustine describes venial sins as "light" but cautions that they pile up: "But do not despise these sins which we call 'light': if you take them for light when you weigh them, tremble when you count them. A number of light objects makes a great mass; a number of drops fills a river; a number of grains makes a heap" (quoted in Catechism of the Catholic Church [CCC], 1863). The *Catechism* says that while venial sin does not break our covenant with God, "Deliberate and unrepented venial sin disposes us little by little to commit mortal sin" (CCC, 1863).

Basic Teaching on Mortal Sin

Mortal sin destroys charity in the heart of man by a grave violation of God's law; it turns man away from God, who is his ultimate end and his beatitude, by preferring an inferior good to him.

For a *sin* to be *mortal* three conditions must together be met: Mortal sin is sin whose object is grave matter and which is committed with full knowledge and deliberate consent.

—*Catechism of the Catholic Church*, 1855, 1857

Daily Mass, Daily Forgiveness

Daily Mass offers us a special opportunity to receive forgiveness for venial sins. Of course we can and should repent of little sins on the spot, but repentance at Mass brings extraordinary graces. (Repentance of mortal sin, however, requires confession at the sacrament of Reconciliation.)

At the very beginning of the liturgy, the priest asks us to prepare ourselves to celebrate the Mass by acknowledging our sins. After a brief pause, he leads us in a prayer of repentance, either the "Lord, Have Mercy" or the *Confiteor*:

> I confess to almighty God
> and to you, my brothers and sisters,
> that I have greatly sinned
> in my thoughts and in my words,
> in what I have done
> and in what I have failed to do,
> through my fault,
> through my fault,
> through my most grievous fault;
> therefore I ask blessed Mary ever-Virgin,
> all the Angels and Saints,
> and you, my brothers and sisters,
> to pray for me to the Lord our God.[1]

This opening rite helps us recognize that no sin, no matter how little or light, is a private matter. All wrongdoing affects others in the Body of Christ. The opening prayer of repentance engages the whole community of the Church in asking the Lord for forgiveness. The rite gives us a special touch of grace.

Purified by the Eucharist

Our participation in the Eucharist, offering Christ's sacrifice with the priest and receiving the Lord in communion, cleanses us of all little sins. For at the consecration, the liturgy proclaims that the Lord's Body is "given up for us" and his Blood is poured out for us and for many "for the forgiveness of sins." "For this reason," says the *Catechism*, "the Eucharist cannot unite us to Christ without at the same time cleansing us of past sins and preserving us from future sins. [As St. Ambrose said:] 'If, as often as his blood is poured out, it is poured out for the forgiveness of sins, I should always receive it, so that it may always forgive my sins. Because I always sin, I should always have a remedy(CCC, 1393).'"

"At the conclusion of the penitential rite the priest prays, 'May almighty God have mercy on us, forgive us our sins, and bring us to everlasting life.' It would be enough for me if Mass ended there, for all I need from God is his mercy and forgiveness and gift of eternal life. Yet there is much more to the Mass— much, much more."

—George M.

The Mass makes present Christ's sacrifice that reconciles us with God. Frequent reception of the Eucharist transmits to us the graces of Calvary. It cleanses us of sin and gives us a fresh start for our Christian life. We should do it every day.

As added benefits, daily Mass both revives our spiritual strength and also galvanizes our will to resist temptation to serious wrongdoing. Venial sins erode our capacity to love God and others, but reception of the Eucharist restores it. At the same time, it loosens our disorderly attachments and enables to break with them (see CCC, 1394). We can receive daily the Lord's help to withstand evil inclinations such as pride, greed, gluttony, and the like.

Go and Sin No More

Repentance which is true and truly from the heart persuades the penitent not to sin any more, not to mix with corrupt people, and not to gape in curiosity at evil pleasures, but to despise things present, cling to things to come, struggle against passions, seek after virtues, be self-controlled in every respect, keep vigil with prayers to God, and shun dishonest gain. It convinces him to be merciful to those who wrong him, gracious to those who ask something of him, ready with all his heart to bend down and help in any way he can, whether by words, actions or money, all who seek his assistance, that through kindness to his fellow-man he might gain God's love in return for loving his neighbor, draw the Divine favor to himself, and attain to eternal mercy and God's everlasting blessing and grace.[2]

—St. Gregory Palamas (1296–1359)

Here's a big blessing of worshipping at daily Mass: the Eucharist fills us with the love of Christ, which preserves us from mortal sin. "The more we share the life of Christ and progress in his friendship, the more difficult it is to break away from him by mortal sin" (CCC, 1395).

Forgiveness, spiritual strength, renewed love, freedom from disorderly attachments and resistance to serious sin are all good reasons to worship at daily Mass. You should build it into your routine. You've got nothing to lose except that pile of little sins.

For Comprehension and Discussion

1. What does it mean to say that a sin is "venial"?

2. How does venial sin differ from mortal sin? What are the three things required to make a sin mortal?

3. In what ways does the Mass help us deal with our little sins?

4. What role does the Eucharist play in cleansing us of sin?

5. How does daily Mass help us to fight sin?

Chapter 4

Taking the Word **to Heart**

Indeed, the word of God is living and effective, sharper than any two-edged sword, penetrating even between soul and spirit, joints and marrow, and able to discern reflections and thoughts of the heart. No creature is concealed from him, but everything is naked and exposed to the eyes of him to whom we must render an account.

—Hebrews 4:12–13

Daily Mass offers the big advantage of immersing us in scripture. During the Liturgy of the Word, the first part of the Mass, we hear the proclamation of two readings and respond to the first with verses from a psalm. The first reading normally comes from the Old Testament, occasionally from the New Testament, and the second from one of the gospels. Some Protestants, whose ears are attuned to the Bible, have even observed that the entire text of the Mass—prayers, songs, readings, responses, the offertory, and eucharistic celebration—draws heavily on scripture. So much for the false notion that Catholics are not biblical!

"Daily Mass helps me put my life in perspective. Why am I here? What do you want me to do, Lord? The Word gives me my daily marching orders. I am in awe every day that the Word is pertinent to what is happening around the world and in my life."

—Christine R.

Over a three-year period, the Liturgy of the Word for Sunday and weekdays covers much of the New Testament—90 percent of Mathew, Mark, Luke, and John, and about 55 percent of the rest (Acts, Letters, and Revelation)—and a smaller portion of the Old Testament.[1] This gives us a double benefit. On one level, we get to see Jesus unfolding and fulfilling God's plan of salvation. Through a year of readings, we walk with him from birth, baptism by John, his public ministry of preaching and healing, his passion, death, and Resurrection.

On another, deeper level, the proclamation of scripture also touches our heart.

The Presence of God

Most Catholics regard the Liturgy of the Eucharist as the highlight of the Mass. It is, for Jesus becomes really present to us on the altar. Bread becomes his Body, wine becomes his Blood. In this miracle of a sacrament, the person of Christ comes to be with us, but Jesus also comes to be with us in the Liturgy of the Word; when the readings are proclaimed at Mass he becomes present to us—really.

The Food of the Soul

The Church has always venerated the divine Scriptures just as she venerates the body of the Lord, since, especially in the sacred liturgy, she unceasingly receives and offers to the faithful the bread of life from the table both of God's word and of Christ's body. She has always maintained them, and continues to do so, together with sacred tradition, as the supreme rule of faith, since, as inspired by God and, committed once and for all to writing, they impart the word of God Himself without change, and make the voice of the Holy Spirit resound in the words of the prophets and Apostles. Therefore, like the Christian religion itself, all the preaching of the Church must be nourished and regulated by Sacred Scripture. For in the sacred books, the Father who is in heaven meets His children with great love and speaks with them; and the force and power in the word of God is so great that it stands as the support and energy of the Church, the strength of faith for her sons, the food of the soul, the pure and everlasting source of spiritual life. Consequently these words are perfectly applicable to Sacred Scripture: "For the word of God is living and active" (Heb. 4:12) and "is able to build you up and give you the inheritance among all who are sanctified" (Acts 20:32; see 1 Thes 2:13).[2]

—Second Vatican Council

The Transforming Power of Scripture

The Church even draws a parallel between the Lord's real presence in the Eucharist and his presence in his Word. If the Lord is really present to us in his Word, we should pay close attention to the readings. Because the Lord himself is speaking to us, we must listen with expectation, even awe, for his words have the power to comfort and change us. That's because God's Word accomplishes what he intends. As the prophet Isaiah, speaking for the Lord, said:

> Yet just as from the heavens
> the rain and snow come down
> And do not return there
> till they have watered the earth,
> making it fertile and fruitful,
> Giving seed to the one who sows
> and bread to the one who eats,
> So shall my word be
> that goes forth from my mouth;
> It shall not return to me empty,
> but shall do what pleases me,
> achieving the end for which I sent it. (Is 55:10–11)

Thus, as we listen to the Liturgy of the Word, God is at work in us. He produces spiritual effects in our lives. He makes us aware of his presence, draws us nearer, tells us of his love, shows compassion for our troubles, offers mercy and forgiveness for our wrongdoing, gives us direction, and so on. The homily, usually quite short at daily Mass, draws the truths from the readings and drives them home with a practical touch.

On the day I wrote this, for example, in the reading from Zechariah (2:5–9, 14–15), God promised the Israelites who returned from exile that he would come and dwell with them. In the gospel, Jesus predicted his death (Lk 9:18–22). The homilist said that the theme of both scriptures was the Lord telling us not to be afraid. The Israelites were not to be anxious for God would be with them, and Jesus was preparing his disciples to face his passion without fear. As I am facing some serious family challenges, being assured that the Lord is with me and that I must not be afraid had a great calming effect on me.

The Goal of Hearing God's Word

The end or fruit of Holy Scripture is not something restricted, but the fullness of eternal happiness. These writings which contain "the message of eternal life" [Jn 6:68 NJB] were written, not only that we might believe in, but also that we might possess that everlasting life in which we shall see, and love, and be fulfilled of all we desire. Then we shall really know that "love of Christ, that surpasses knowledge," and thus "be filled with the utter fullness of God" [Eph 3:19 NJB]. This is the fullness to which the divine Scriptures would lead us, as is truly said in the words of the Apostle quoted above. Such, then, must be our goal and our intent in studying and in teaching the Scriptures, and also in hearing them.[3]

—St. Bonaventure (1218–1274)

Just hearing the proclamation of God's Word evokes in us the faith to receive the graces he offers to renew and strengthen our lives. As St. Paul explained to the Christians at Rome, "faith comes from what is heard, and what is heard comes through the word of Christ" (Rom 10:17).

Messages from God

God wants to communicate with us daily through the readings and the homily. We should expect that he has a personal message for us and listen carefully. Maybe he wants to speak to us about something that worries us. Maybe he wants to give us direction for our life. Consider the example of St. Antony (251–356). He had inherited a large estate, but wondered if he should imitate the apostles, who left all to follow Jesus. With this on his mind, he went to Mass at a nearby church. St. Athanasius (ca. 297–373), his biographer, says:

> It happened the Gospel was being read, and he heard the Lord saying to the rich man, "If you wish to be perfect, go, sell what you have and give to [the] poor, and you will have treasure in heaven. Then come, follow me." Antony, as though the passage had been read on his account, went out immediately from the church, and gave his family possessions to the villagers—they were three hundred acres, productive and very fair—so that they should be no more a burden upon himself and his sister. And all the rest that was movable he sold, and having got together much money he gave it to the poor, reserving a little however for his sister's care.[4]

Antony spent the next eighty years as a monk in the desert, praying and counseling many visitors. His example, broadcast by Athanasius's widely read biography, inspired the development of monasticism in the Western Church.

You may never hear at Mass such a radical, life-changing message, but you may hear the Lord telling you to make a change in your behavior. For example, once I heard God speak to me in this verse from a psalm: "The Lord is gracious and merciful, slow to anger and abounding in love" (Ps 145:8). He was encouraging me to treat my wife with more kindness and to curb my anger.

"In time of need or worry there is always a word of comfort from the daily scripture. As the Lord says, 'Come to me all you who labor and are overburdened and I will give you rest.' It's remarkable how the daily readings correlate to your daily situations."

—Mario F.

Catholic author and speaker Matthew Kelly suggests that we carry a small notebook to Mass. Then, when the Holy Spirit strikes us with a thought that grabs our attention, we can jot it down and consider it prayerfully later. Reviewing those notes as they accumulate will convince us that God really loves us and cares for our lives.

At daily Mass I expect to experience the Lord's presence in the Liturgy of the Word and hear him speak to me a word that will touch my heart. Why don't you join me? Bring your notebook.

For Comprehension and Discussion

1. Describe the Liturgy of the Word. (What are its elements and in what order do they occur?)

2. What double benefit do we enjoy from the daily readings from the New Testament?

3. What does it mean to say that God's Word accomplishes what he intends?

4. Why should we listen expectantly to the proclamation of the Word?

5. What are the daily and long-term advantages of noting down what God is saying to you at Mass?

Chapter 5

Frequent **Intercession**

And I tell you, ask and you will receive;
seek and you will find; knock and the door
will be opened to you. For everyone who
asks, receives; and the one who seeks, finds;
and to the one who knocks, the door will
be opened. What father among you would
hand his son a snake when he asks for a
fish? Or hand him a scorpion when he asks
for an egg? If you then, who are wicked,
know how to give good gifts to your
children, how much more will the Father
in heaven give the Holy Spirit to those who
ask him?

—Luke 11:9–13

From the earliest days of the Church, the Liturgy of the
Word closed with a time of universal prayer. For example,
in AD 155, St. Justin wrote to the Roman emperor describing the pattern of Christian worship. He said that after the
readings and the homily, we offer "hearty prayers in common for ourselves . . . and for all others in every place."[1]
This practice reflected the teaching of St. Paul, who called

us to offer "supplications, prayers, petitions, and thanks-givings" for everyone, especially those in authority (see 1 Tm 2:1–2).

Today, two millennia later, the liturgy follows the same arrangement. Typically at the time of intercession, called the Prayer of the Faithful, we pray for the needs of the Church, for public authorities and the salvation of the whole world, for those burdened by any kind of difficulty, and for the local community.[2] We also usually intercede for the sick and for those recently deceased.

A Model Prayer of the Faithful

Priest's Introduction

Dear brothers and sisters, may every prayer of our heart be directed to God the Father almighty, for it is his will that all humanity should be saved and come to knowledge of the truth.

Intentions

1) For the whole Christian people, the abundance of divine goodness, let us pray to the Lord.

Response: Lord, hear our prayer.

2) For the peoples of all the world, that the Lord may preserve harmony among them, let us pray to the Lord.

Lord, hear our prayer.

3) For those who hold public office, let us call upon the power of the Lord.

Lord, hear our prayer.

4) For all who are oppressed by any kind of need, that the Lord may grant them relief, let us pray to the Lord.

Lord, hear our prayer.

5) For the repose of the souls of the faithful departed, let us pray to the Lord.

Lord, hear our prayer.

6) For ourselves and our own community that the Lord may receive us as a sacrifice acceptable to himself.

Lord, hear our prayer.

Priest's Prayer

O God, our refuge and our strength and the source of all devotion, hear the prayers of your Church and grant, we pray, that what we ask for in faith we may truly obtain. Through Christ our Lord. Amen.[3]

My friends who worship at daily Mass at St. Mary Magdalen Church regard the intercessions as a highlight. Bringing their hot-button needs to the Lord is a prime reason for their attendance. When Fr. Ed, our ninety-year-old associate pastor, asks, "What else shall we pray for?" the congregation announces a chorus of requests: "For my Aunt Cathy who starts chemo today"; "that more young men will discern vocations to the priesthood"; "for all the unemployed of the parish that they will find work"; and so on.

The Power behind Our Intercession

One of my friends told me that experiencing the Prayers of the Faithful gives her confidence to face her problems. "I feel," she said, "that sisters and brothers are supporting me just like the men who supported Moses when he was praying for Joshua." She was referring to the famous story in Exodus. As long as Moses held up his arms in prayer, Joshua prevailed in the battle. When Moses grew tired, Aaron and Hur supported his arms, giving Joshua the power to win the war (see Ex 17:8–13).

"I am always more peaceful after I attend Mass. I know God is God and I am not. He has everything in his hands."

—Marita M.

Interceding Like Jesus and the Holy Spirit

Intercession is a prayer of petition which leads us to pray as Jesus did. He is the one intercessor with the Father on behalf of all men, especially sinners (cf. Rom 8:34, 1 Jn 2:1; 1 Tm 2:5–8). He is "able for all time to save those who draw near to God through him, since he always lives to make intercession for them" (Heb 7:25).The Holy Spirit

"himself intercedes for us . . . and intercedes for the saints according to the will of God" (Rom 8:26–27).
—*Catechism of the Catholic Church*, 2634

The spiritual power of the Prayer of the Faithful comes from Jesus, who prays with us. Scripture says that Jesus is "able for all time to save those who draw near to God through him, since he always lives to make intercession for them" (Heb 7:25). Remarkable, isn't it? Jesus spends his heaven praying for us. As Paul declared in his letter to the Romans, "It is Christ [Jesus] who died, rather, was raised, who also is at the right hand of God, who indeed intercedes for us" (Rom 8:34).

J. Peter Sartain, the Archbishop of Seattle, reflected on Jesus' intercession and identified the love that empowers it:

> Jesus' eternal prayer of intercession is so perfect that even from the cross he prayed for those who harmed him. It is precisely there—on the cross—where the love behind his intercession reveals itself. Jesus longs for all people to come with him to the Father; he seeks only the best for all, and he gave his life for all. His gift of himself on the cross and his eternal prayer of intercession for us are different aspects of the one love he has for us, and his eternal intercession always points to trust in his Father's mercy.[4]

My friends at the 7 a.m. Mass and I have experienced the graces of Jesus' intercession. Recently, for example, I prayed for a friend of mine whose wife had filed a spurious injunction against him. At the Prayer of the Faithful I asked the Lord to persuade her to drop it. Had the judge enforced the injunction, my friend might have lost his license to practice law. To my delight, at the hearing later that morning she dropped it.

The Lord has said "yes" to our prayers for successful open heart surgeries, knee and hip replacements, for a man who lost a job one day and found another the next, and more. Sometimes he has said "not yet"—we are still waiting for him to heal Frank's back so he can return to daily Mass, and God had something better for Dotty, a regular, whom he took home after she had suffered for a year with leukemia.

"If I have a family member or friend who is in need, I remember him or her at Mass. When I have promised to pray for someone, I bring the intention before the altar. There are many instances of difficulties over which I have no control, but if I petition the Lord at Mass, I feel I can offer some actual assistance."

—Jackie L.

Trust and Expectant Faith

Sometimes we wonder why our intercession seems to fail. St. Robert Bellarmine (1542–1621) says that may be because we do not live in God's presence and only turn to him when things go bad. Commenting on "You who dwell in the shelter of the Most High" (Ps 91:1), he explains why some prayers may be answered and others not:

> Why is it that some men implore divine assistance without receiving it, and seem to put their trust in God without being protected by him? The reason is that they do not really dwell in the aid of the Most High, nor take shelter under the providence of God as in their Father's house. They rather make sporadic dashes to it in time of trouble, as they do to a tree when there is a sudden shower. It is therefore very necessary for us to get into the way of always and instinctively turning to God.[5]

Your Will Be Done

And we have this confidence in him, that if we ask anything according to his will, he hears us. And if we know that he hears us in regard to whatever we ask, we know that what we have asked him for is ours.

—1 John 5:14–15

Instinctively turning to God and trusting him for everything positions us to approach God for our needs. It is in this spirit of trust that we can exercise our faith and expect the Lord to grant our requests. These two

dispositions of the heart—trust and expectant faith—
prepare us for effective intercession.

For Comprehension and Discussion

1. Why do you think the Prayer of the Faithful is also
   called the Universal Prayer?

2. When the priest-celebrant asks for your intercessions,
   what might you pray for?

3. Why can we say that Jesus gives power to the Prayer
   of the Faithful?

4. What explanation does St. Robert Bellarmine give for
   failed intercessory prayer? What must we do to correct
   the failure?

5. How do trust and expectant faith work together for
   effective intercession?

Chapter 6

Offering Ourselves **to God**

> Love proves itself by deeds, so how am I
> to show my love? . . . The only way I can
> prove my love is by scattering flowers, and
> these flowers are every little sacrifice, every
> glance and word, and doing the least of
> actions for love. I wish both to suffer and to
> find joy through love.[1]
>
> —St. Thérèse of Lisieux (1873–1897)

If we had gathered with first-century Christians for Mass,
we would have brought with us bread, wine, and other
goods, which could be given to those in need. At the preparation of gifts, formerly called the offertory—which from
earliest times has opened the Liturgy of the Eucharist—
we would have processed to the altar and have given our
gifts to the priest. Here's how Archbishop Fulton J. Sheen
imagined the scene:

> If we went to the Holy Sacrifice in the early Church, we
> would have brought to the altar each morning some
> bread and some wine. The priest would have used one
> piece of that unleavened bread and some of that wine for
> the sacrifice of the Mass. The rest would have been put

41

aside, blessed, and distributed to the poor. . . . Why do we bring bread and wine or its equivalent to the Mass? We bring bread and wine because these two things, of all things in nature, most represent the substance of life. Wheat is as the very marrow of the ground, and the grapes its very blood, both of which give us the Body and Blood of life. In bringing those two things, which give us life, nourish us, we are equivalently bringing ourselves to the Sacrifice of the Mass.[2]

Life and All Creation

The bread and wine that the priest and we offer carry great symbolic value. They signify life itself, all creation, and ourselves. They stand for the life I celebrate on my early morning walk—my neighbor's newly sodded lawn, my vibrant Roubellini palm, the wasps congregating under the eaves of my roof, and the neighborhood cat waiting on my porch for her morning snack. I acknowledge the Lord's gift of my own life at my morning prayer and at the offertory. I thank him for creating me, for giving me a human nature, and for sustaining and providing for me.

Pope Francis Offers a Life

As Pope Francis was leaving the cathedral of St. Sebastian in Rio de Janeiro on Saturday [July 27, 2013, at World Youth Day] following Mass with the bishops and priests, he met a couple who presented to him their own newly-born daughter who was born anencephalic (without a brain). Normally the baby would have died at birth, but she was still alive. The parents did not wish to abort their child even though an abortion would have been allowed legally for such a case. The parents wished to welcome the gift of life.

During the final Mass of World Youth Day, Pope Francis welcomed this child during the offertory procession of the Mass as a gesture of welcome and offering of a life to God.[3]

—Thomas Rosica

During the Liturgy of the Eucharist, Christ takes up the bread and wine representing all creation and presents them to the Father. We are talking here about *all* creation. The cosmos of 300 billion trillion stars; seven billion human beings on the planet and counting; the innumerable wonders of this beautiful earth—the mountains, valleys, deserts, rivers, seas and all that's in them. As St. John Paul II said, "the world which came forth from the hands of God the Creator now returns to him redeemed by Christ."[4] It startles me that a little piece of bread and an ounce of wine carry such enormous weight and significance!

"Daily Mass contributes to my life in Christ by helping me put my life in perspective. Why am I here? What do you want me to do, Lord? I offer my petitions with the offering of bread and wine through the priest."

—Caroline R.

We Offer Ourselves

Once, before Mass, I asked my associate pastor, Fr. Ed, to pray for an intention. He said, "I will put you in the chalice." That stuck in my memory; so now at Mass I acknowledge that I am in both the bread and the wine that will be offered. As Archbishop Sheen explained, "We are therefore present at each and every Mass under the appearance of bread and wine."

Co-offering the Mass with Christ

We are therefore present at each and every Mass under the appearance of bread and wine. . . . We are not passive spectators as we might be watching a spectacle in a theater, but we are co-offering our Mass with Christ. If any picture adequately describes our role in this drama it is this: There is a great cross before us on which is stretched the great Host, Christ. Round about the hill of Calvary are our small crosses on which we, the small hosts, are to be offered. When our Lord goes to His Cross we go to our little crosses, and offer ourselves in union with Him, as a clean oblation to the heavenly Father.

At that moment we literally fulfill to the smallest detail the Savior's command: Take up your cross daily and follow Me. In doing so, He is not asking us to do anything He has not already done Himself.[5]

—Archbishop Fulton J. Sheen

Not only are we contained in the substance of the offering, but we also offer the bread and wine with the priest. Archbishop Sheen again says: "We are not passive spectators as we might be watching a spectacle in a theater, but we are co-offering our Mass with Christ." In this prayer, which the priest prays silently, he engages our participation in the offering: "With humble spirit and contrite heart may we be accepted by you, O Lord, and may our sacrifice in your sight this day be pleasing to you, Lord God."[6]

I like it when a priest prays this prayer in a stage whisper, acknowledging my collaboration in the offering. Then, of course, the priest invites us to pray aloud that his sacrifice *and ours* will be acceptable to God, and we make our co-offering with these words: "May the Lord accept the sacrifice at your hands for the praise and glory of his name, for our good and the good of all his holy Church."[7]

"During Mass I can offer praise and thanks for what God has given us all and particularly me. I seek support for needs through beseeching Christ. I seek guidance in all matters of choice from the Holy Spirit, and at Mass I ask for strengthening of faith and hope in the future."

—Dick E.

Giving Ourselves to God

At daily Mass, the preparation of the gifts gives us an opportunity to renew our decision to follow Jesus. It gives us a chance to surrender our heart more fully to the Lord. When we offer ourselves with the bread and wine, we are saying "yes" to Jesus' command to take up our cross daily and follow him (see Lk 9:23).

Surrendering Our Heart to the Lord

Don't think that you must do great things to show our Lord that you love him. No, great things are good when God presents them. But let's offer our little things to his goodness with great love and great submissiveness, and the recompense will be in proportion to these two things.

Nowhere in Scripture does the Lord say: My son, my daughter, give me your head, your arms, your life, but only, "My child, give me your heart" [see Mt 22:37]. Whoever has a person's heart has the whole person. The heart is the seat of love. "When I have your heart," says the Lord, "I will set my love on it. And I will even make my love dwell in it, and all the rest will follow as a consequence."[8]

—St. Jane de Chantal (1572–1641)

My surrender at the Mass spills over into my daily routine. During the day, I like to occasionally affirm my discipleship with this little prayer of Cardinal Joseph Mercier (1851–1926):

> Oh, Holy Spirit, beloved of my soul, I adore you. Enlighten me, guide me, strengthen me, console me. Tell me what I should do; give me your orders. I promise to submit myself to all that you desire of me and to accept all that you permit to happen to me. Let me only know your will.[9]

I recommend this prayer of submission as a follow-up to Mass. It lightens our daily load because, with it, we entrust everything to the will of God.

For Comprehension and Discussion

1. Why can we say that the bread and wine represent all life and creation?

2. How do the bread and wine stand for us?

3. In what way does Archbishop Sheen illustrate our co-offering the Mass with Christ?

4. How might we deliberately offer ourselves to the Lord at Mass?

5. How can our self-offering at Mass spill over into our daily life?

Chapter 7

Offering the
Eternal Sacrifice

At the Last Supper, on the night when
He was betrayed, our Savior instituted
the eucharistic sacrifice of His Body and
Blood. He did this in order to perpetuate
the sacrifice of the Cross throughout the
centuries until He should come again,
and so to entrust to His beloved spouse,
the Church, a memorial of His death and
resurrection: a sacrament of love, a sign of
unity, a bond of charity, a paschal banquet
in which Christ is eaten, the mind is filled
with grace, and a pledge of future glory is
given to us.[1]

—Second Vatican Council

Every time we enter our parish church for Mass we dip
our fingers in holy water and make the sign of the cross.
We often do it casually without much thought, but it is a
very important gesture and we should do it intentionally.
It reminds us of our baptism, which united us to God and

made us members of the Church. With it, we are declaring that, as members of the Body of Christ, we share in his priesthood. The sign demonstrates that we are authorized to participate in the liturgy, offering with Christ his eternal sacrifice. This is an enormous privilege that we should exercise often, daily if possible.

The Last Supper and the Eucharist

On the night before he was to die, Jesus chose to share a final meal with his beloved disciples. Together they celebrated Passover, the feast which represented for Jews a perpetual memorial of their deliverance from bondage in Egypt (see Ex 12). The annual celebration reminded them that every family had sacrificed a lamb and splashed its blood on their doorposts, so that the angel coming to slay the first borns of the Egyptians would pass over their houses.

At this Last Supper with his friends, Jesus transformed Passover into the sacrificial meal of the New Covenant we call the Eucharist. Jesus was replacing the Passover lamb with himself as "the Lamb of God, who takes away the sins of the world" (Jn 1:29). Here's how the gospel of Matthew describes the event: "While they were eating, Jesus took bread, said the blessing, broke it, and giving it to his disciples said, 'Take and eat; this is my body.' Then he took a cup, gave thanks, and gave it to them, saying, 'Drink from it, all of you, for this is my blood of the covenant, which will be shed on behalf of many for the forgiveness of sins'" (Mt 26:26–28). St. Paul, in the earliest account of the founding of the Eucharist, says that Jesus directed his disciples to do these things "in remembrance of me" (see 1 Cor 11:23–26).

Now, more than two thousand years later, that remembrance continues at every Mass. At the consecration of the bread and wine, we experience the re-presentation of Christ's eternal sacrifice. Jesus' death and resurrection are not locked in the past, but rather—breaking the barriers of time and space—they are made present to us in the Eucharist.

Jesus Really Present

In his daily Mass homilies, Fr. Ed often points to the altar and says, "In a few minutes, Jesus will be really present there in his Body and Blood, soul and divinity." He means, of course, that the bread and wine we offer will become the Body and Blood of Christ.

"I worship at daily Mass because I believe that, at Mass, heaven touches earth and earth touches heaven, and I want to be there for this meal of bread and wine—Christ's Body and Blood."

—Gladys B.

Here's how the transformation occurs. The priest repeats the Lord's own words, "This is my body," and "this is my blood." While the appearances of bread and wine remain, their substance or hidden reality changes into the Body and Blood of Christ. Because the priest's words *transform* the *substance* of these elements, at the suggestion of St. Thomas Aquinas, Catholics describe this miraculous change as "transubstantiation."

Be wary of imagining that we are talking about mere symbols. As St. Cyril declared, "Since Christ himself described the bread to us in these words, 'This is my body,' who will dare dispute it? And since he has emphatically said, 'This is my blood,' who will waver in the slightest and say it is not his blood?"[2]

Adore This Wondrous Presence

Of the glorious Body telling, O my tongue, its mystery sing;

And the Blood, all price excelling, which for this world's ransoming

In a noble womb once dwelling, he shed forth, the Gentiles' King.

At the Last Great Supper seated, circled by his brethren's band,

All the Law required, completed, in the feast its statutes planned,

To the Twelve himself he provided their food with his own hand.

Therefore, we, before it bending, this great sacrament adore;

Types and shadows have their ending in the new rite ever more;

Faith, our outward sense amending, maketh good defects before.[3]

—St. Thomas Aquinas

We Offer Christ's Sacrifice

At the offertory, we have the great privilege of giving ourselves to God with the bread and wine. After the consecration, we have the even greater privilege of offering with Jesus his eternal sacrifice and sacrificing ourselves with him.

On the altar of the cross, Jesus offered himself to his Father as he then was—in his physical body. Now on our altar, Jesus offers himself to his Father as he now is—in his whole body, the Body of Christ, the Church. That should thrill us because not only do we have the honor of offering Christ's sacrifice, we also get to sacrifice ourselves united to him as members of his body.

"Daily Mass is crucial to my spiritual life, and when I attend Mass after having missed for some days, it's as if I'm returning home. The mystery of the Mass, where the God of creation comes to me, is astounding and awesome and shakes me through."

—George E.

The signs of the sacrament declare this reality and make it effectively present because they indicate our inclusion in the Eucharistic sacrifice: bread made from many grains of wheat ground into flour and wine pressed from many grapes symbolize Christ's corporate body as it now is, with him as the head and we the members (see 1 Cor 10:16–17).

The Sacrifice of the Body of Christ

What happened there on the Cross that day is happening now in the Mass, with this difference: On the Cross the Savior was alone; in the Mass He is with us. Our Lord is now in heaven at the right hand of the Father, making intercession for us. He therefore can never suffer again in His human nature. How then can the Mass be the re-enactment of Calvary? How can Christ renew the Cross? He cannot suffer again "in His own human nature" which is in heaven enjoying beatitude, but He can suffer again in "our human natures." He cannot renew Calvary in His "physical body," but He can renew it in His "Mystical Body"—the Church. The Sacrifice of the Cross can be re-enacted provided we give Him our body and our blood, and give it to Him so completely that as His own, He can offer Himself anew to His heavenly Father for the redemption of His Mystical Body, the Church.

So the Christ goes out into the world gathering up other human natures who are willing to be Christs. In order that our sacrifices, our sorrows, our Golgothas, our crucifixions, may not be isolated, disjointed, and unconnected, the Church collects them, harvests them, unifies them, coalesces them, masses them, and this massing of all our sacrifices of our individual human natures is united with the Great Sacrifice of Christ on the Cross in the Mass.[4]

—Archbishop Fulton J. Sheen

In the liturgy, the priest prays a series of intercessions that lead up to the climax of our participation in the sacrifice. "Therefore, Lord," he prays, "as we now celebrate the memorial of our redemption . . . we offer you his Body and Blood, the sacrifice acceptable to you which brings salvation to the whole world."[5] After several additional prayers, we get to voice our ratification of the sacrifice. The priest lifts the chalice of Christ's Blood and the paten containing his Body and says:

> Through him, and with him, and in him,
>
> O God, almighty Father,
>
> in the unity of the Holy Spirit,
>
> all glory and honor is yours,
>
> now and forever.[6]

We affirm our agreement with the Great "Amen!" which we should do intentionally with faith, joy, and gusto.

For Comprehension and Discussion

1. What is the significance of our signing ourselves with holy water as we enter the church?

2. How did Jesus transform the Passover meal into the Eucharist?

3. What does it mean that the Mass re-presents Christ's sacrifice?

4. What happens to make bread and wine become the Body and Blood of Christ?

5. Why can we say that, at Mass, *we* offer Christ's sacrifice and sacrifice ourselves with him?

Chapter 8

Our Daily **Bread**

The Father in heaven urges us, as children
of heaven, to ask for the bread of heaven.
[Christ] himself is the bread who, sown in
the Virgin, raised up in the flesh, kneaded in
the Passion, baked in the oven of the tomb,
reserved in churches, brought to altars,
furnishes the faithful each day with food
from heaven.[1]

—St. Peter Chrysologus (ca. 380–450)

In my sophomore year at college I discovered *Of Sacraments and Sacrifice* by Clifford Howell, S.J., a remarkable
book about the sacraments, especially the Eucharist. Lights
came on in my nineteen-year-old brain when I read Fr.
Howell's explanation of the sacrifice of the Mass. He
described our self-offering and receiving Communion at
Mass as an exchange of gifts. When a young man, he said,
gives his girlfriend a gift of candy, she does not just put it
away on a shelf. Rather she eats a piece and offers some to
him. Something similar, but of a much higher order, happens at Mass. Led by the priest, we offer ourselves with

Christ to the Father. At Communion, God gives us a share in the Body and Blood of Christ, which we have offered.

The Exchange of Gifts

If the young man who gave a present to his girlfriend gets something back, shall not we who have given a present to our God get something back? Of course we do! God offers back to us a share of what we gave to him, just as the girl offers back to the young man a share of what he gave her. God says, "Have some!" And so we come to the altar and eat of the sacrificial gift. That is Communion. It is the return gift from God—the natural and obvious sequel to our giving a gift to him. *Exchange of gifts!*[2]

—Clifford Howell, S.J.

Completing the Sacrifice

Jesus founded the Eucharist at a Passover meal, presenting himself as the new Lamb of God. Just as the Passover sacrifice was not complete until each family consumed the lamb, so the sacrifice of the Mass is not complete until we partake of the Body and Blood of the Lord. "In both the Old Testament and the ancient Jewish tradition," says theologian Brant Pitre, "the sacrifice of the Passover lamb was not completed by its death. It was completed by a meal, by *eating the flesh of the lamb* that had been slain. Therefore, if Jesus saw himself as the new lamb, then it makes sense that he would speak of his blood being poured out and command the disciples to eat his flesh."[3]

Jesus' declaration at the Last Supper that the bread was his Body and the wine his Blood must have been an "Aha!" moment for his disciples. The meaning of his mysterious words to the crowd at Capernaum finally dawned on them: "Unless you eat the flesh of the Son of Man and drink his blood, you do not have life within you. Whoever eats my flesh and drinks my blood has eternal life, and I will raise him on the last day. For my flesh is true food, and my blood is true drink" (Jn 6:53–55).

Jesus' promise, too, must have struck the disciples. Eating his body and drinking his blood would bring the wonderful gift of eternal life.

Feeding on Jesus

The Jews quarreled among themselves, saying, "How can this man give us [his] flesh to eat?" Jesus said to them, "Amen, amen, I say to you, unless you eat the flesh of the Son of Man and drink his blood, you do not have life within you. Whoever eats my flesh and drinks my blood has eternal life, and I will raise him on the last day. For my flesh is true food, and my blood is true drink. Whoever eats my flesh and drinks my blood remains in me and I in him. Just as the living Father sent me and I have life because of the Father, so also the one who feeds on me will have life because of me. This is the bread that came down from heaven. Unlike your ancestors who ate and still died, whoever eats this bread will live forever."

—John 6:52–58

Give Us Today Our Daily Bread

F. J. Sheed says that every kind of life has its own food. He explains that material food nourishes bodily life and mental food nourishes intellectual life. "But," he says, "*the life we are now concerned with is Christ living in us; the only possible food for it is Christ.*"[4] That's why Jesus gave us this assurance: "My flesh is true food, and my blood is true drink" (Jn 6:55). Feeding on Jesus sustains our life in him.

When Jesus taught us to pray, he instructed us to ask the Father to "Give us today our daily bread" (Mt 6:11). On one level, we are asking God to provide food for our bodies. We count on him for our daily sustenance, but that petition of the Our Father has a deeper meaning. From the earliest days, the Church has understood that "daily bread" referred to the Eucharist. Jesus wants us to feed on his Body and Blood every day. F. J. Sheed says, "The Blessed Eucharist is *the* sacrament. Baptism exists *for* it, all the others are enriched by it. The whole being is nourished by it. It is precisely food, which explains why it is the one sacrament meant to be received daily. Without it, one petition of the *Our Father*—'Give us this day our daily bread'—lacks the fullness of its meaning."[5]

Eating Christ's Body and drinking his Blood has a marvelous effect on us: we become what we eat! "When we receive Communion," said the bishops of the United States, "we need to remember that we are not changing Christ into ourselves. Jesus is transforming us into himself."[6] Daily Communion magnifies our share in Christ's life and makes us more like him. "The Eucharist," said St. Augustine, "is our daily bread. The power belonging to this divine food makes it a bond of union. Its effect is then understood as unity, so that, gathered into his Body and made members of him, we may become what we receive."[7]

The Power of Receiving Communion

The Body and Blood of Christ are given to us so that we ourselves will be transformed in our turn. We are to become the Body of Christ, his own Flesh and Blood. We all eat the one bread, and this means that we ourselves become one. In this way, adoration . . . becomes union. God no longer simply stands before us as the One who is totally Other. He is within us, and we are in him. His dynamic enters into us and then seeks to spread outwards to others until it fills the world.[9]

—Pope Benedict XVI

A Remedy for Sin

A close reflection on our Christian life reveals a disturbing paradox. Even though Communion unites us more fully to Christ, our evil inclinations still slide us into sin. We slip into venial sins, the little pardonable ones—behaviors like irritability, fudging on the truth, or giving the cold shoulder. No need to worry, though—receiving the Body and Blood of Christ is not only food for the soul, it is also medicine, a remedy for venial sins and an inoculation against mortal sins.

As our love for Jesus in the Eucharist increases, he helps us to resist sin. The *Catechism* explains that "[as] bodily nourishment restores lost strength, so the Eucharist strengthens our charity, which tends to be weakened in daily life; and this living charity *wipes away venial sins* (cf. Council of Trent [1551] . . .). By giving himself to us, Christ revives our love and enables us to break our disordered attachments to creatures and root ourselves in him (CCC, 1394). . . . By the same charity that it enkindles in us, the Eucharist *preserves us from future mortal sins*" (CCC, 1395).

Communion forgives venial sins and strengthens us to fight against falling into serious sin. Remember that we should not receive Communion if we have committed mortal sin and have not yet been forgiven in the Sacrament of Reconciliation. Thus, St. Paul warns against receiving Christ's Body and Blood when we have fallen into some grievous sin: "Therefore whoever eats the bread or drinks the cup of the Lord unworthily will have to answer for the Body and Blood of the Lord" (1 Cor 11:27–29).

A Eucharistic Community

For the past eight years, I have worshiped daily at the 7 a.m. Mass at our local parish. I gather with the same people every morning; we have become an informal community. Our celebration of the Eucharist, especially our sharing in the Body and Blood of Christ, has banded us together. As St. Paul says, "The cup of blessing that we bless, is it not a participation in the blood of Christ? The bread that we break, is it not a participation in the body of Christ? Because the loaf of bread is one, we, though many, are one body, for we all partake of the one loaf" (1 Cor 10:16–17).

Many of my brothers and sisters have told me how our morning community has touched their lives. "I know the people I go to daily Mass with," says Mike. "I know their stories. It moves me to be with them. After Mass people mingle and chat and share what's been going on; they ask for prayers and ask about my family. It feels like family. It is the place where I am accepted and loved and respected because they know my story, too."

Celebrating the Daily Mass Community

I delight in seeing the same elderly couples each morning, holding hands in prayer just as they did on their wedding day. I'm encouraged by our ninety-year-old priest who celebrates Mass with deep reverence even after sixty years and thousands of liturgies. I'm thrilled that people know our family's names, ask about our children, and inquire about our spiritual life. I used to constrain my "spiritual time" to a half-hour alone, where I would read my Bible and pray all by myself, but I've since realized the great value of praying, worshiping, singing, and communing with others. A community of faith strengthens its members as they edify and encourage each other to new heights.

—Brandon V.

Like many others, Ann says, "The daily Mass community is special. We know if someone is missing, who is sick or hurting, and we have a prayer community of fellow believers to support them. It is like a second family to me. Each of us has a burden we carry, and, together, we can share the weight and help each other carry our crosses."

Participating in our daily Mass community has given us a real experience of the Body of Christ.

Perhaps this chapter more than the others will persuade you to consider worshiping at daily Mass. You will receive immeasurable benefits from receiving the Body and Blood of Jesus every day: nourishment for your soul, a closer union with Jesus, transformation in Christ, a remedy for sin, the experience of community, and, best of all, eternal life.

For Comprehension and Discussion

1. In what way is the Eucharist an exchange of gifts?

2. Why does the nature of the sacrifice of the Mass require that we eat Christ's Body and drink his Blood?

3. What does it mean that, when we receive Communion, we become what we eat?

4. Why can we say that Communion is a remedy for sin?

5. What are the benefits of receiving Communion? Which benefits do you find most appealing?

Chapter 9

Equipped for the
Day's Service

Receiving the Eucharist daily gives me
my spiritual fuel and strengthens me to
overcome day-to-day obstacles. Daily Mass
helps me to start my day off in communion
with Christ. It helps me to wake up and be
more alert to what God has in store for me.

—David M.

The 7 a.m. daily liturgy is drawing to a close. None of my
friends are gathering up their booklets, keys, or purses. No
one is putting on his jacket. All are paying close attention
to the concluding rites. They seem to be anticipating the
words that will launch their day's activities. After the priest
prays the prayer after Communion and gives us the final
blessing, he will dismiss us with this exhortation: "Go in
peace, glorifying the Lord with your life."[1]

This charge reminds us how worshiping at Mass has
equipped us for our day. We have been doubly nourished.
We have fed on the Word of God and on the Body and
Blood of Christ.

The Liturgy of the Word builds us up every day. The proclamation of scripture shows us how to live, corrects our sinfulness, gives us hope, and more. One of the readings often convicts me. On the day I wrote this, for example, the deacon commented in the homily on the compassion Jesus showed to a deaf man. He said Jesus healed him privately so as not to embarrass him before the crowd (see Mk 7:31–37). He exhorted us to relate to others with similar care and sensitivity.

Participating in the Eucharist truly empowers us for our day. First thing in the morning, Jesus comes to us in Communion. His Real Presence within us trumps our worries, calms our fears, and strengthens us to face our challenges. Here's what some members of my 7 a.m. Mass community say:

> **Elizabeth S.:** Hearing God's word read and reflected on by the homilist plus receiving the Body and Blood of Christ give me "food for the journey."

> **Mike M.:** Mass helps me to know who I am and why I am. I feel centered. Communion fortifies and sustains me for whatever is coming in the day ahead. I have more confidence, more patience, and more concern for the people that I encounter when I go to daily Mass.

> **Helen S.:** At daily Mass, the Lord has given me courage and hope to face the daily distractions and problems that our families and our country are confronting.

> **Antoney M.:** Jesus gives me the strength to face my challenges that come at me as a small business owner. I always ask Jesus to give me faith and I know he has walked with me step-by-step every day. I can see his footprints all around me. I started a small business in 2008, and without Jesus in my life I would not have

made it. There are times I look back and wonder how I survived the last five years, but without the faith that fills me up at the daily Mass, I would not have made it.

Carol K.: I worship at daily Mass because it fulfills me. I actually started going after my mother passed away suddenly. It helped me through it. I felt the closeness of Jesus, knowing he was there giving me the comfort that I needed. I need to give Jesus thanks for each and every day as he is always with me.

Bill D.: I can commune with Jesus directly and intimately—everyday! Word and sacrament take on a special, intimate meaning and stay with me throughout the day. Every day brings its challenges, but the incredible graces I receive at daily Mass give me the strength to face those challenges in a more Christ-like way.

Worshiping at daily Mass has very practical consequences. There, the Lord gives us the grace to fight traffic on our commute, gets us ready to clean the house, prepares us to meet and serve feisty customers, helps us perform the multi-tasks of single-parenting, and more.

Strengthened to Serve

Just before Jesus ascended to his Father, he commissioned the eleven apostles to go and make disciples of all nations (see Mt 28:18). His command has echoed through two millennia, expanding its scope to include all the baptized. Now that Great Commission telescopes into the dismissal of contemporary disciples at every Mass. Another form of the closing exhortation directs us to "Go and announce the Gospel of the Lord."[2]

The word *Mass* carries that evangelistic thrust. It derives from *"Ite, missa est,"* the dismissal of the Latin liturgy, which means "go, you are sent." The liturgy involves far more than spending time in worship. It also engages us in continuing the work of Christ.

Working with Christ

The word *liturgy* originally meant a "public work" or a "service in the name of/on behalf of the people." In Christian tradition it means the participation of the People of God in "the work of God" (cf. Jn 17:4). Through the liturgy Christ, our redeemer and high priest, continues the work of our redemption in, with, and through his Church.
—*Catechism of the Catholic Church*, 1069

Daily Mass primes us for our service in the Body of Christ. The Lord gives us the grace we need to accomplish what he calls us to do in the Church and the world. For example, some of my friends find strength for their service in the parish at the 7 a.m. Mass. As sacristans, John, Peggy, Al, and Tom handle all the details for Mass; Suzanne, Mario, Gladys, and Harry serve as extraordinary ministers of the Eucharist; Joan and Antoney take Communion to the sick; Drew teaches at the parish school; Ann and George are leaders in the social justice commission; and Joe heads up the parish's Habitat for Humanity program. The list could go on. In short, daily Mass fuels our parish's life and ministry.

The Lord also engages us in his work of evangelization. By our baptism, we have the duty and privilege of drawing others to Christ and the Church. We do this in our ordinary relationships by the way we live and what we say. Worshiping at Mass enhances our ability to evangelize by giving us the joy and ardor that others find attractive.

Missionary Disciples

The new evangelization calls for personal involvement on the part of each of the baptized. Every Christian is challenged, here and now, to be actively engaged in evangelization; indeed, anyone who has truly experienced God's saving love does not need much time or lengthy training to go out and proclaim that love. Every Christian is a missionary to the extent that he or she has encountered the love of God in Christ Jesus: we no longer say that we are "disciples" and "missionaries," but rather that we are always "missionary disciples."[3]

—Pope Francis

Evangelization reaches more people with witness than with teaching. We want to intrigue people with our Christian way of living—with our joyful, kind, and upright behavior. "Through this wordless witness," said Pope Paul VI in a remarkable Apostolic Exhortation, "Christians stir up irresistible questions in the hearts of those who see how they live: Why are they like this? Why do they live in this way? What or who is it that inspires them? Why are they in our midst? Such a witness is already a silent proclamation of the Good News and a very powerful and effective one."[4]

"At the right moment, usually when someone gives us an opening, we must give words to our witness. We must tell them in our own words how we came to know the Lord and commit our life to him. Again, Pope Paul VI explains: "The Good News proclaimed by the witness of life sooner or later has to be proclaimed by the word of life. There is no true evangelization if the name, the teaching, the life, the promises, the kingdom and the mystery of Jesus of Nazareth, the Son of God are not proclaimed."[5]

Daily Mass helps us get ready for this important service. The proclamation of the scripture gives us words, and receiving the Lord in the Eucharist gives us the grace for good witness.

Father has just dismissed my friends and me from Mass, charging us to proclaim the Gospel with our lives. Sonya is off to home school her four children; Carol, Brandon, Christine, and Bill are going to their respective offices; Henry is heading to visit Jim, a very sick parishioner; Kathleen is taking her three little ones to a play date with friends; and I'm due home for a conference call in fifteen minutes. The Lord we received at Mass is going with us to guide and strengthen us.

For Comprehension and Discussion

1. In what ways do the words of the dismissal affect our daily lives?

2. Why can we say that the word "Mass" carries an evangelistic thrust?

3. How does daily Mass prime us for our service in the Body of Christ?

4. How does daily Mass prepare you for your service? If you do not yet worship at daily Mass, how do you think it might affect your life and service?

5. Why does Paul VI say that evangelization must involve both word and witness?

Afterword

The little book that you have just read declares truths that demand action. You have considered with me the ways daily Mass benefits us. I expect that they have caught your attention and may have intrigued you.

Now I invite you to act. I urge you to build Mass into your daily routine. If family, work, or study duties allow you to reserve about an hour a day (that's a half-hour for Mass and fifteen minutes to and from church), you should decide to do it. If your life circumstances will not permit attending Mass every day, look for ways of doing it once or twice a week. You might choose to worship at daily Mass for a liturgical season such as Advent or Lent. (A friend of mine decided a dozen years ago to attend Mass every day in Lent and he has never stopped the practice.)

Think about the following questions. They will help you reach a good decision.

- In what ways would daily Mass help me? How would it contribute to my life?
- What duties or circumstances prevent me from attending Mass daily?
- What might I do to rearrange my affairs so that I can fit daily Mass into my routine?

May these considerations draw you to participate in Christ's sacrifice every day.

May you find yourself there in a community of friends who will encourage and support you.

May the experience of daily Mass draw you ever closer to Christ and make you more and more like him.

Appendix I
Prayers before Mass

Prayer of St. Ambrose

Lord Jesus Christ,
I approach your banquet table in fear and trembling,
for I am a sinner, and dare not rely on my own worth,
but only on your goodness and mercy.
I am defiled by many sins in body and soul,
and by my unguarded thoughts and words.
Gracious God of majesty and awe,
I seek your protection, I look for your healing.
Poor troubled sinner that I am, I appeal to you, the fountain of all mercy.
I cannot bear your judgment, but I trust in your salvation.

Lord, I show my wounds to you and uncover my shame before you.
I know my sins are many and great, and they fill me with fear,
but I hope in your mercies, for they cannot be numbered.
Lord Jesus Christ, eternal king, God and man, crucified for mankind,
look upon me with mercy and hear my prayer, for I trust in you.
Have mercy on me, full of sorrow and sin,
for the depth of your compassion never ends.

Praise to you, saving sacrifice,
offered on the wood of the cross for me and for all mankind.

Praise to the noble and precious blood,
    flowing from the wounds of my crucified Lord Jesus
    Christ
and washing away the sins of the whole world.
Remember, Lord your creature, whom you have
    redeemed with your blood

I repent of my sins, and I long to put right what I have
    done.
Merciful Father, take away all my offenses and sins;
    purify me in body and soul,
and make me worthy to taste the holy of holies.
    May your Body and Blood , which I intend to receive,
    although I am unworthy,
be for me the remission of my sins, the washing away of
    my guilt,
the end of my evil thoughts, and the rebirth of my better
    instincts.
May it incite me to do the works pleasing to you and
    profitable to my health in body and soul,
and be a firm defense against the wiles of my enemies.
    Amen.[1]

Prayer of St. Thomas Aquinas

Almighty and ever-living God,
I approach the sacrament
of your only-begotten Son
our Lord Jesus Christ,
I come sick to the doctor of life,
unclean to the fountain of mercy,
blind to the radiance of eternal light,
and poor and needy to the Lord
of heaven and earth.

Lord, in your great generosity,
heal my sickness,
wash away my defilement,
enlighten my blindness, enrich my poverty,
and clothe my nakedness.
May I receive the bread of angels,
the King of kings and Lord of lords,
with humble reverence,
with the purity and faith,
the repentance and love,
and the determined purpose
that will help to bring me to salvation.
May I receive the sacrament
of the Lord's Body and Blood,
and its reality and power.

Kind God,
may I receive the Body
of your only-begotten Son,
our Lord Jesus Christ,
born from the womb of the Virgin Mary,
and so be received into his mystical body
and numbered among his members.

Loving Father,
as on my earthly pilgrimage
I now receive your beloved Son
under the veil of a sacrament,
may I one day see him face to face in glory,
who lives and reigns with you forever. Amen.[2]

Celebrating Christ's Body and Blood
A Devotion Based on the Liturgy of the Hours

O God, come to my assistance.
—O Lord, make haste to help me.

Blessed be Jesus in the most holy Sacrament of the Altar!
—Blessed be his holy Name, now and forever!

Hymn

Sing, my tongue, the Saviour's glory,
Of his Flesh the mystery sing;
Of the Blood, all price exceeding,
Shed by our immortal King,
Destined, for the world's redemption,
From a noble womb to spring.

Of a pure and spotless Virgin
Born for us on earth below,
He, as Man with man conversing,
Stay'd, the seeds of truth to sow;
Then he closed in solemn order
Wondrously his life of woe.

On the night of that Last Supper,
Seated with his chosen band,
He the Paschal victim eating,
First fulfils the Law's command;
Then, as Food to his Apostles
Gives himself with his own hand.

Word made Flesh, the bread of nature
By his word to Flesh he turns;
Wine into his Blood he changes:
What though sense no change discerns?
Only be the heart in earnest,

Faith her lesson quickly learns.

Therefore, we, before it bending,
This great Sacrament adore;
Types and shadows have their ending
In the new rite evermore:
Faith, our outward sense amending,
Maketh good defects before.

Honor, laud, and praise addressing
To the Father and the Son,
Might ascribe we, virtue, blessing,
And eternal benison:
Holy Ghost, from both progressing,
Equal laud to Thee be done. Amen.[3]

Psalm 116: A Sacrifice of Praise

Antiphon: I will offer a sacrifice of praise and call on the name of the Lord.

How can I repay the Lord
for all the great good done for me?
I will raise the cup of salvation
and call on the name of the Lord.
I will pay my vows to the Lord
in the presence of all his people.
Dear in the eyes of the Lord
is the death of his devoted.

Lord, I am your servant,
your servant, the child of your maidservant;
you have loosed my bonds.
I will offer a sacrifice of praise
and call on the name of the Lord.

I will pay my vows to the Lord
in the presence of all his people,

In the courts of the house of the Lord,
in your midst, O Jerusalem.
Hallelujah!

Glory to the Father, and the Son
And to the Holy Spirit;
As it was in the beginning, is now,
And will be forever. Amen

Antiphon: I will offer a sacrifice of praise and call on the name of the Lord.

Psalm Prayer

O Lord, I thank you for all your gifts to me. I honor your Son, Jesus Christ and promise to embrace his living presence in the holy sacrament of the altar, now and forever. Amen.

Reading: John 6:52–58

The Jews quarreled among themselves, saying, "How can this man give us [his] flesh to eat?" Jesus said to them, "Amen, amen, I say to you, unless you eat the flesh of the Son of Man and drink his blood, you do not have life within you. Whoever eats my flesh and drinks my blood has eternal life, and I will raise him on the last day. For my flesh is true food, and my blood is true drink. Whoever eats my flesh and drinks my blood remains in me and I in him. Just as the living Father sent me and I have life because of the Father, so also the one who feeds on me will have life because of me. This is the bread that came down from heaven. Unlike your ancestors who ate and still died, whoever eats this bread will live forever."

Response

As often as you eat this bread and drink the cup,
—You will proclaim the Lord's death until he comes.

Canticle of the Church

We praise you O God, we acknowledge you to be the
      Lord;
all the earth now worships you, the Father everlasting.
To you all angels cry aloud, the heavens and all the
      powers therein;
to you cherubim and seraphim continually cry:
            Holy, holy, holy Lord, God of Hosts
            heaven and earth are full of the majesty of your
            glory.
The glorious company of the apostles praise you,
The goodly fellowship of the prophets praise you,
The noble army of martyrs praise you.

The holy Church throughout all the world acknowledges
      you:
            the Father of an infinite majesty,
            your adorable, true, and only Son,
            also the Holy Spirit, the counselor.
You are the King of glory, O Christ.
You are the everlasting Son of the Father.
When you took upon yourself to deliver us,
you humbled yourself to be born of a virgin.
When you had overcome the sting of death, you opened
      the kingdom of heaven to all believers.
You sit at the right hand of God in the glory of the
      Father.
We believe that you will come to be our judge.
We therefore pray you help your servants,
whom you have redeemed with your precious blood.

Make them to be numbered with your saints in glory
    everlasting.[4]

Closing Prayer

Lord Jesus Christ, You gave us the Eucharist as the
memorial of your passion and death. May our worship
of your Body and Blood help us to experience the salvation you won for us and the peace of the kingdom where
you live with the Father and the Holy Spirit, one God
forever and ever. Amen.

Appendix II
Prayers after Mass

Soul of Christ (*Anima Christi*)

Soul of Christ, sanctify me.
Body of Christ, save me.
Blood of Christ, inebriate me.
Water from the side of Christ, wash me.
Passion of Christ, strengthen me.
O good Jesus, hear me.
Within your wounds, hide me.
Separated from you let me never be.
From the malignant enemy, defend me.
At the hour of death, call me.
To come to you, bid me,
That I may praise you in the company
Of your Saints, for all eternity. Amen.

Prayer of St. Thomas Aquinas

Lord, Father all-powerful and ever-living God, I thank
you.
For even though I am a sinner and your unprofitable
servant,
not because of my worth, but in the kindness of your
mercy,
you have fed me with the precious Body and Blood of
your Son, our Lord Jesus Christ

I pray that this Holy Communion
may not bring me condemnation and punishment
but forgiveness and salvation.
May it be a helmet of faith and a shield of good will.

May it purify me from evil ways and put an end to my
    evil passions.
May it bring me charity and patience, humility and
    obedience,
and growth in power to do good.
May it be my strong defense against all my enemies,
    visible and invisible,
and the perfect calming of all my evil impulses, bodily
    and spiritual.
May it unite me more closely to you, the one true God
and lead me safely through death to everlasting happi-
    ness with you.
And I pray that you will lead me, a sinner, to the
    banquet
where you, with your Son and Holy Spirit,
are true and perfect light, total fulfillment, everlasting
    joy,
gladness without end, and perfect happiness to your
    saints.
Grant this through Christ our Lord. Amen.

Prayer of Saint Bonaventure

Pierce, O most Sweet Lord Jesus, my inmost soul with
the most joyous and healthful wound of your love.
Pierce my soul with true, serene, and most holy apostolic
charity, that it may ever languish and melt with love and
longing for you. May my soul yearn for you and faint for
your courts, and may it long to be dissolved and to be
with you.

Grant that my soul may hunger after you, the bread of
angels, the refreshment of holy souls. May it hunger for
our daily and supersubstantial bread, having all sweetness and savor and every delight of taste. Let my heart
ever hunger after and feed upon you, upon whom the

angels desire to look. May my inmost soul be filled with
the sweetness of your savor. [1]
May it ever thirst after you, the fountain of life, of wisdom and knowledge and eternal light, the torrent of
pleasure, the richness of the house of God.

May my heart ever draw close to you, seek you, find
you, run to you, attain you, meditate upon you and
speak of you. May it do all things to the praise and glory
of your name, with humility and discretion, with love
and delight, with ease and affection, and with persever-
ance unto the end. May you alone be ever my hope, my
entire assurance, my riches, my delight, my pleasure, my
joy, my rest and tranquility, my peace, my sweetness, my
fragrance, my sweet savor, my food, my refreshment, my
refuge, my help, my wisdom, my portion, my possession
and my treasure. In you may my mind and my heart
be fixed and firmly rooted immovably henceforth and
forever. Amen. [1]

Prayer of St. Ignatius of Loyola

Lord Jesus Christ, take all my freedom,
my memory, my understanding, and my will.
All that I have and cherish
you have given me.
I surrender it all to be guided by your will.
Your grace and your love
are enough for me.
Give me these, Lord Jesus,
and I ask for nothing more. Amen.[2]

Thanksgiving for Christ's Body and Blood
A Devotion Based on the Liturgy of the Hours

O God, come to my assistance.
—O Lord, make haste to help me.

Blessed be Jesus in the most holy Sacrament of the Altar!
—Blessed be his holy Name, now and forever!

Hymn

Hidden God, devoutly I adore thee,
Truly present underneath these veils:
All my heart subdues itself before thee,
Since it all before thee faints and fails.
Not to sight, or taste, or touch be credit,
Hearing only do we trust secure;
I believe, for God the Son hath said it–
Word of Truth that ever shall endure.
On the Cross was veiled thy Godhead's splendor,
Here thy manhood lieth hidden too;
Unto both alike my faith I render,
And, as sued the contrite thief, I sue.
Though I look not on thy wounds with Thomas,
thee, my Lord, and thee, my God, I call:
Make me more and more believe thy promise,
Hope in thee, and love thee over all.
O Memorial of my Saviour dying,
Living Bread that givest life to man;
May my soul, its life from thee supplying,
Taste thy sweetness, as on earth it can.
Deign, O Jesus, pelican of heaven,
Me, a sinner, in thy Blood to lave,
To a single drop of which is given
All the world from all its sin to save.

Contemplating Lord, thy hidden presence,
Grant me what I thirst for and implore,
In the revelation of thine essence
To behold thy glory evermore.[3]

Psalm 23: The Table of the Lord

Antiphon: You set a table before me.

The Lord is my shepherd;
there is nothing I lack.
In green pastures he makes me lie down;
to still waters he leads me;
he restores my soul.

He guides me along right paths
for the sake of his name.
Even though I walk through the valley of the shadow of
    death,
I will fear no evil, for you are with me;
your rod and your staff comfort me.

You set a table before me
in front of my enemies;
You anoint my head with oil;
my cup overflows.
Indeed, goodness and mercy will pursue me
all the days of my life;
I will dwell in the house of the Lord
for endless days.
Glory to the Father, and the Son
And to the Holy Spirit;
As it was in the beginning, is now,
And will be forever. Amen.

Antiphon: You set a table before me.

Psalm Prayer

Father, by the waters of baptism you authorized me to participate in Christ's eternal sacrifice. And at the table of the altar you have fed me on his Body and Blood. For these great blessings I give thanks to you, the Father almighty, with the Holy Spirit and Jesus Christ, the Lord. Amen.

Reading: 1 Corinthians 11:23–26

For I received from the Lord what I also handed on to you, that the Lord Jesus, on the night he was handed over, took bread, and, after he had given thanks, broke it and said, "This is my body that is for you. Do this in remembrance of me." In the same way also the cup, after supper, saying, "This cup is the new covenant in my blood. Do this, as often as you drink it, in remembrance of me." For as often as you eat this bread and drink the cup, you proclaim the death of the Lord until he comes.

Response

You sent them bread from heaven,
—Having in itself every delight.

Canticle of the Church

We praise you O God, we acknowledge you to be the
    Lord;
all the earth now worships you, the Father everlasting.
To you all angels cry aloud, the heavens and all the pow-
    ers therein;
to you cherubim and seraphim continually cry:
        Holy, holy, holy Lord, God of Hosts
        heaven and earth are full of the majesty of your
        glory.
The glorious company of the apostles praise you,
The goodly fellowship of the prophets praise you,

The noble army of martyrs praise you.

The holy Church throughout all the world acknowledges
you:
>the Father of an infinite majesty,
>your adorable, true, and only Son,
>also the Holy Spirit, the counselor.

You are the King of glory, O Christ.
You are the everlasting Son of the Father.
When you took upon yourself to deliver us,
you humbled yourself to be born of a virgin.
When you had overcome the sting of death, you opened
the kingdom of heaven to all believers.
You sit at the right hand of God in the glory of the
Father.
We believe that you will come to be our judge.
We therefore pray you help your servants,
whom you have redeemed with your precious blood.
Make them to be numbered with your saints in glory
everlasting.[4]

Closing Prayer

Lord Jesus Christ, who under this wonderful sacrament
have left us a memorial of your passion: grant us so to
reverence the sacred mysteries of your Body and Blood,
that we may ever realize within ourselves the fruit of
your redemption. You live and reign forever with the
Father in the unity of the Holy Spirit, one God forever
and ever. Amen.

Appendix III
The General Roman Calendar Adapted for the United States of America

Adapted from the *Roman Missal*, "General Roman Calendar," 121-132. UPPERCASE type indicates solemnities and feasts, which are specified in parentheses. Standard type indicates a memorial. *Italics* indicate an optional memorial.

January

1   MARY, THE HOLY MOTHER OF GOD (Solemnity)

2   St. Basil and St. Gregory Nazianzen

3   *The Most Holy Name of Jesus*

4   St. Elizabeth Ann Seton [USA]

5   St. John Neumann [USA]

6   St. André Bessette [USA]

7   *St. Raymond of Penyafort*

13 St. Hilary of Poitiers

17 St. Anthony of Egypt

20 *St. Fabian and St. Sebastian*

21 St. Agnes

22 Day of Prayer for the Legal Protection of Unborn Children [USA]

23 St. Vincent of Saragossa [USA]

24 St. Francis de Sales

25 THE CONVERSION OF ST. PAUL (Feast)

26 St. Timothy and St. Titus

27 *St. Angela Merici*

28 St. Thomas Aquinas

31　St. John Bosco

Sunday between January 2 and January 8: THE EPIPH-
ANY OF THE LORD (Solemnity) [USA]

Sunday after January 6: THE BAPTISM OF THE LORD
(Feast)

February

2　THE PRESENTATION OF THE LORD (Feast)

3　*St. Blaise; St. Ansgar*

5　St. Agatha

6　St. Paul Miki and Companions

8　*St. Jerome Emiliani; St. Josephine Bakhita*

10　St. Scholastica

11　*Our Lady of Lourdes*

14　St. Cyril and St. Methodius

17　*The Seven Holy Founders of the Servite Order*

21　*St. Peter Damian*

22　THE CHAIR OF ST. PETER (Feast)

23　St. Polycarp

March

3　*St. Katharine Drexel* [USA]

4　*St. Casimir*

7　St. Perpetua and St. Felicity

8　*St. John of God*

9　*St. Frances of Rome*

17　*St. Patrick*

18　*St. Cyril of Jerusalem*

19　ST. JOSEPH (Solemnity)

23　*St. Turibius of Mogrovejo*

25　THE ANNUNCIATION OF THE LORD (Solemnity)

April

2   *St. Francis of Paola*
4   *St. Isidore of Seville*
5   St. Vincent Ferrer
7   St. John Baptist de la Salle
11 St. Stanislaus
13 *St. Martin I*
21 *St. Anselm*
23 *St. George; St Adalbert*
24 *St. Fidelis of Sigmaringen*
25 ST. MARK (Feast)
28 *St. Peter Chanel; St. Louis Grignon de Montfort*
29 St. Catherine of Siena
30 *St. Pius V*

May

1   St. Joseph the Worker
2   St. Athanasius
3   ST. PHILIP AND ST. JAMES (Feast)
10 St. Damien de Veuster [USA]
12 *St. Nereus and St. Achilleus; St. Pancras*
13 *Our Lady of Fatima*
14 ST. MATTHIAS (Feast)
15 *St. Isidore* [USA]
18 *St. John I*
20 *St. Bernardine of Siena*
21 *St. Christopher Magallanes*
22 *St. Rita of Cascia*

25 *St. Bede the Venerable; St. Gregory VII; St. Mary Magdalene de Pazzi*

26 St. Philip Neri

27 *St. Augustine of Canterbury*

31 VISITATION OF THE BLESSED VIRGIN MARY (Feast)

June

1   St. Justin

2   *St. Marcellinus and St. Peter*

3   St. Charles Lwanga and Companions

5   St. Boniface

6   *St. Norbert*

9   *St. Ephrem*

11 St. Barnabas

13 St. Anthony of Padua

19 *St. Romuald*

21 St. Aloysius Gonzaga

22 *St. Paulinus of Nola; St. John Fisher and St. Thomas More*

24 THE NATIVITY OF ST. JOHN THE BAPTIST (Solemnity)

27 *St. Cyril of Alexandria*

28 St. Irenaeus

29 ST. PETER AND ST. PAUL (Solemnity)

30 *First Martyrs of the Church of Rome*
    Friday after the Second Sunday after Pentecost: THE MOST SACRED HEART OF JESUS (Solemnity)

July

1   Bl. Junípero Serra [USA]

3   ST. THOMAS (Feast)

4   Independence Day [USA]

5   St. Anthony Zaccaria; *St. Elizabeth of Portugal* [USA]

6   *St. Maria Goretti*
9   *St. Augustine Zhao Rong and Companions*
11 St. Benedict
13 *St. Henry*
14 St. Kateri Tekawitha [USA]
15 St. Bonaventure
16 *Our Lady of Mt. Carmel*
18 *St. Camillus de Lellis* [USA]
20 *St. Apollinaris*
21 *St. Lawrence of Brindisi*
22 St. Mary Magdalene
23 *St. Bridget*
24 *St. Sharbel Makhlūf*
25 ST. JAMES (Feast)
26 St. Joachim and St. Anne
29 St. Martha
30 *St. Peter Chrysologus*
31 St. Ignatius Loyola

August

1   St. Alphonsus Liguori
2   *St. Eusebius of Vercelli; St. Peter Julian Eymard*
4   St. John Vianney
5   *The Dedication of the Basilica of St. Mary Major*
6   THE TRANSFIGURATION OF THE LORD (Feast)
7   *St. Sixtus II and Companions; St. Cajetan*
8   St. Dominic
9   *St. Teresa Benedicta of the Cross*
10 ST. LAWRENCE (Feast)
11 St. Clare
12 *St. Jane Frances de Chantal*

13 *St. Pontian and St. Hippolytus*

14 St. Maximilian Kolbe

15 THE ASSUMPTION OF THE BLESSED VIRGIN MARY
    (Solemnity)

16 *St. Stephen of Hungary*

19 *St. John Eudes*

20 St. Bernard

21 St. Pius X

22 The Queenship of the Blessed Virgin Mary

23 *St. Rose of Lima*

24 ST. BARTHOLOMEW (Feast)

25 *St. Louis; St. Joseph Calasanz*

27 *St. Monica*

28 St. Augustine

29 The Passion of St. John the Baptist

September

3   St. Gregory the Great

8   THE NATIVITY OF THE BLESSED VIRGIN MARY
    (Feast)

9   St. Peter Claver [USA]

12 *The Most Holy Name of Mary*

13 St. John Chrysostom

14 THE EXALTATION OF THE HOLY CROSS (Feast)

15 Our Lady of Sorrows

16 St. Cornelius and St. Cyprian

17 *St. Robert Bellarmine*

19 *St. Januarius*

20 St. Andrew Kim Taegŏn, St Paul Chŏng Ha-sang and
    Companions

21 ST. MATTHEW (Feast)

23 St. Pius of Pietrelcina
26 *St. Cosmas and St. Damian*
27 St. Vincent de Paul
28 *St. Wenceslas; St. Lawrence Ruiz and Companions*
29 ST. MICHAEL, ST. GABRIEL, AND ST. RAPHAEL (Feast)
30 St. Jerome

October

1   St. Therésè of the Child Jesus
2   The Holy Guardian Angels
4   St. Francis of Assisi
6   *St. Bruno; Bl. Marie Rose Durocher* [USA]
7   Our Lady of the Rosary
9   *St. Denis and Companions; St. John Leonardi*
14 *St. Callistus*
15   St. Teresa of Jesus
16 *St. Hedwig; St. Margaret Mary Alacoque*
17 St. Ignatius of Antioch
18 ST. LUKE (Feast)
19 St. John de Brébeuf, St. Isaac Jogues, and Companions [USA]
20 *St. Paul of the Cross* [USA]
22 St. John Paul II
23 *St. John of Capistrano*
24 *St. Anthony Mary Claret*
28 ST. SIMON AND ST. JUDE (Feast)

November

1   ALL SAINTS (Solemnity)
2   ALL SOULS' DAY

3   *St. Martin de Porres*
4   St. Charles Borromeo
9   THE DEDICATION OF THE LATERAN BASILICA
    (Feast)
10 St. Leo the Great
11 St. Martin of Tours
12 St. Josaphat
13 *St. Frances Xavier Cabrini* [USA]
15 *St. Albert the Great*
16 *St. Margaret of Scotland; St. Gertrude*
17 St. Elizabeth of Hungary
18 *The Dedication of the Basilicas of St. Peter and St. Paul; St.*
    Rose Philippine Duchesne [USA]
21 The Presentation of the Blessed Virgin Mary
22 St. Cecilia
23 *St. Clement I; St. Columban; Bl. Miguel Agustín Pro* [USA]
24 *St. Andrew Dũng-Lac and Companions*
25 *St. Catherine of Alexandria*
30 ST. ANDREW (Feast) Last Sunday of Ordinary Time:
    OUR LORD JESUS CHRIST, KING OF THE UNIVERSE
    (Solemnity)

December
3   St. Francis Xavier
4   *St. John Damascene*
6   *St. Nicholas*
7   St. Ambrose
8   THE IMMACULATE CONCEPTION OF THE
    BLESSED VIRGIN MARY (Solemnity) [USA]
9   *St. Juan Diego Cuauhtlatoatzin*
11 *St. Damasus I*

12 OUR LADY OF GUADALUPE (Feast) [USA]

13 St. Lucy

14 St. John of the Cross

21 *St. Peter Canisius*

23 *St. John of Kanty*

25 THE NATIVITY OF THE LORD (CHRISTMAS) (Solemnity)

26 ST. STEPHEN (Feast)

27 ST. JOHN (Feast)

28 THE HOLY INNOCENTS (Feast)

29 *St. Thomas Becket*

31 *St. Sylvester I*

Sunday within the Octave of the Nativity; or if there is no Sunday, December 30: THE HOLY FAMILY OF JESUS, MARY, AND JOSEPH (Feast)

Appendix IV
Holy Days of Obligation in the United States of America

January 1: The Solemnity of Mary, Mother of God

Thursday of the Sixth Week of Easter: The Solemnity of the Ascension

August 15: The Solemnity of the Assumption of Blessed Virgin Mary

November 1: The Solemnity of All Saints

December 8: The Solemnity of the Immaculate Conception

December 25: The Nativity of Our Lord Jesus Christ

Appendix V
Liturgical Feasts of Mary

Among the most prominent Marian feast days in the ordinary Roman Catholic Calendar are the following.

January 1: Mary, Mother of God

January 8: Our Lady of Prompt Succor

February 2: Purification of the Virgin

February 11: Our Lady of Lourdes

March 25: Annunciation by Archangel Gabriel (May be moved to either [1] the day before Palm Sunday, should any part of Holy Week fall on March 25; or [2] to the Monday after the second Sunday of Easter, should either the Friday or Saturday of Holy Week, or any part of Easter Week, fall on March 25.)

April 26: Our Lady of Good Counsel

May 1: Queen of Heaven

May 13: Our Lady of Fatima

May 24: Mary Help of Christians

May 31: Visitation of the Blessed Virgin Mary

June 27: Our Lady of Perpetual Help

July 16: Our Lady of Mount Carmel

August 2: Our Lady of the Angels

August 5: Dedication of the Basilica of Saint Mary Major

August 15: Assumption into Heaven

August 21: Our Lady of Knock

August 22: Queenship of Mary

August 22: Black Madonna of Częstochowa

August 31: The Virgin Mary Mediatrix

September 8: Nativity of the Blessed Virgin Mary

September 12: The Most Holy Name of the Blessed Virgin Mary

September 15: Our Lady of Sorrows

September 19: Our Lady of La Salette

September 24: Our Lady of Walsingham, Feast of Our Lady of Ransom

October 7: Most Holy Rosary

November 16: Our Lady of Mercy

November 21: Presentation of Mary

December 8: Immaculate Conception

December 12: Our Lady of Guadalupe

One day after Ascension of Jesus: Our Lady of the Apostles

One day after Pentecost: Our Lady of Holy Church

Nine days after Corpus Christi: Immaculate Heart of Mary

Resources

For Worship

Daily Roman Missal. 3rd ed. Woodridge, IL: Midwest Theological Forum, 2011. Available at OSV.com.

The Word Among Us. This a Catholic devotional magazine based on the daily Mass readings. Available at www.wau. org.

For Study

Catechism of the Catholic Church. 2nd ed. Available at http:// www.usccb.org/beliefs-and-teachings/what-we-believe/ catechism/catechism-of-the-catholic-church/epub/index. cfm.

Dubruiel, Michael. *The How to Book of the Mass.* Huntington, IN: Our Sunday Visitor, 2007.

Ghezzi, Bert. *The Heart of Catholicism.* Notre Dame, IN: Ave Maria Press, 2104.

Hahn, Scott. *The Lamb's Supper.* New York: Doubleday, 1999.

Vaghi, Peter J. *The Sacraments We Celebrate.* Notre Dame, IN: Ave Maria Press, 2009.

Notes

Preface

1. Curtis Martin is the president and founder of the Fellowship of Catholic University Students (FOCUS; www.focus.org). The monstrance is the vessel the Church uses to display the consecrated eucharistic host during eucharistic adoration or benediction of the Blessed Sacrament.

1. Every Day with Jesus

1. Vatican Council II, *Constitution on the Sacred Liturgy* (Sacrosanctum Concilium) *Promulgated by His Holiness Pope Paul VI, December 4, 1963*, 102.

2. Ibid.

3. St. Augustine, "Sermon on the Ascension of the Lord," in *The Office of Readings According to the Roman Rite*, trans. The International Commission on English in the Liturgy (Boston: Daughters of St. Paul, 1983), 617–618.

4. Janet Schaeffler, O.P., *The Liturgical Year*, (Huntington, IN: Our Sunday Visitor, 2007), 4.

5. *United States Catechism for Adults* (Washington, DC: United States Conference of Catholic Bishops, 2006), 173.

6. "Universal Norms on the Liturgical Year and the Calendar, 39," quoted in *Daily Roman Missal* ed. James Socias (Woodridge, IL: Midwest Theological Forum, 2004), 2.

7. Benedict XVI, "Homily for Midnight Mass, Solemnity of the Nativity of the Lord, December 24, 2006," accessed April 24, 2014, http://www.vatican.va/holy_father/benedict_xvi/homilies/2006/documents/hf_ben-xvi_hom_20061224_christmas_en.html.

8. *Ceremonial of Bishops*, cited in the *Daily Roman Missal*, 422. The *Ceremonial of Bishops* is a book that describes the liturgical services to be performed by bishops of the Latin Rite of the Roman Catholic Church.

9. James Quinn, S.J., *Praise for All Seasons: The Hymns of James Quinn, S.J.* (Pittsburgh, PA: Selah), 18.

10. *Ceremonial of Bishops*, cited in the *Daily Roman Missal*, 838.

2. Honoring the Saints

1. Vatican Council II, *Constitution on the Sacred Liturgy*, 104.

2. See Appendix III: The General Roman Calendar Adapted for the United States of America, for the Cycle of Saints.

3. Frank J. Sheed, *Theology for Beginners* (Ann Arbor, MI: Servant Books, 1981), 115.

4. St. Philip Neri, accessed November 3, 2013, http://www.liturgialatina.org/oratorian/maxims.htm.

5. "December 31: Saint Sylvester I, Pope," *Roman Missal*, (Collegeville, MN: Liturgical Press, 2011), 1027.

6. James Martin, S.J., *My Life with the Saints* (Chicago, IL: Loyola Press, 2006), 374–375.

7. St. Bernard of Clairvaux, "Sermon," in *The Office of Readings According to the Roman Rite*, trans. The International Commission on English in the Liturgy (Boston: Daughters of St. Paul, 1983), 1614–1615.

3. Daily Repentance

1. "The Introductory Rites" and "Penitential Act," *Roman Missal*, 513–521.

2. St. Gregory Palamas, "Homily Twenty-Eight," *The Homilies of Saint Gregory Palamas*, Vol. II, trans. Christopher Veniamin (South Canaan, PA: St. Tikhon's Seminary Press, 2004). Homily available at http://oca.orlg/reflections/writings-of-the-saints/sermon-on-the-feast-of-sts.-peter-and-paul-leaders-of-the-apostles.

4. Taking the Word to Heart

1. Felix Just, S.J., *The Catholic Lectionary Website*, accessed September 26, 2013, http://catholic-resources. org/Lectionary/Overview.htm.

2. Vatican Council II, *Dogmatic Constitution on Divine Revelation* (Dei Verbum), *Promulgated by His Holiness Pope Paul VI, December 4, 1963*, 21.

3. St. Bonaventure, "Prologue to *Breviloquium*," quoted in *Christian Readings* (New York: Catholic Book Publishing Company, 1972), I (Year 2), 217.

4. Adapted from St. Athanasius, *Life of Antony*, accessed September 25, 2013, http://www.fordham.edu/halsall/basis/vita-antony.asp.

5. Frequent Intercession

1. Adapted from St. Justin, *Apology*, 1, 65, and 67 passim, accessed October 9, 2013, http://www.ccel.org/ccel/schaff/anf01.viii.ii.lxv.html.

2. "The Universal Prayer," in *General Instruction of the Roman Missal*, accessed October 9, 2013, http://www.usccb. org/prayer-and-worship/the-mass/order-of-mass/liturgy-of-the-word/universal-prayer.cfm.

3. Adapted from the *Roman Missal*, Appendix V, 1461, http://forum.musicasacra.com/forum/uploads/FileUpload/de/714b01a182c172a98696a39eb0ff26.pdf.

4. J. Peter Sartain, *Journey to the Heart of Jesus* (Huntington, IN: Our Sunday Visitor, 2014), 116–117.

5. James Brodrick, *Robert Bellarmine: Saint and Scholar* (Westminster, MD: The Newman Press, 1961), 41.

6. Offering Ourselves to God

1. St. Thérèse of Lisieux, *Story of a Soul*, trans. John Clarke (Washington, DC: ICS Publications, 1996), 162.

2. Fulton J. Sheen, "The Offertory," *Calvary and the Mass*, available through Sancta Missa's online "Tutorial on

the Latin Mass According to the 1962 Missale Romanum," accessed October 25, 2013, http://www.sanctamissa.org/en/resources/books/calvary/the-offertory.html.

3. Thomas Roscica, "Offering the gift of life—Special offertory at Closing Mass of WYD Rio," *salt+light* (blog), Salt and Light Media, July 28, 2013, http://saltandlighttv.org/blog/world-youth-day/offering-the-gift-of-life-special-offertory-at-closing-mass-of-wyd-rio.

4. St. John Paul II, *"Ecclesia de Eucharistia,"* Encyclical Letter, Promulgated April 17, 2003, 8.

5. Sheen, "The Offertory," *Calvary and the Mass.*

6. "Liturgy of the Eucharist," *Roman Missal*, 529.

7. Ibid.

8. St. Jane de Chantal, *St. Jane de Chantal: Her Exhortations, Conferences, Instructions, and Retreat* (Bristol: Sisters of the Visitation, 1888), 410.

9. Joseph Mercier, "Prayer to the Holy Spirit," in *A Catholic Prayer Book,* accessed October 27, 2013, http://www.catholicity.com/prayer/prayer-to-the-holy-spirit-3.html.

7. Offering the Eternal Sacrifice

1. Vatican Council II, *Constitution on the Sacred Liturgy,* 47.

2. St. Cyril of Jerusalem, *"Mystagogical Catechesis,* Sermon 4, 1–2," in *A Catholic Book of Hours and Other Devotions,* ed. William G. Storey (Chicago, IL: Loyola Press, 2007), 219–220.

3. St. Thomas Aquinas, *Pange Lingua Gloriosi,* quoted in Vol. 3 of *The Roman Breviary,* trans. John Marquess of Bute, K.T. (Edinburgh and London: William Blackwood and Sons, 1908), 227.

4. Sheen, "Consecration," *Calvary and the Mass.*

5. Catholic Church and James Socías, Eucharistic Prayer IV, *Daily Roman Missal*.

6. Ibid.

8. Our Daily Bread

1. St. Peter Chrysologus, "Sermon 67," quoted in CCC, 2837.

2. Adapted from Clifford Howell, S.J., *Of Sacraments and Sacrifice* (Collegeville, MN: The Liturgical Press, 1952) 130 (emphasis in original).

3. Brant Pitre, *Jesus and the Jewish Roots of the Eucharist* (New York, NY: Image, 2011), 74 (emphasis in original).

4. Sheed, *Theology for Beginners*, 153 (emphasis in original).

5. Ibid., 155 (emphasis in original).

6. *United States Catholic Catechism*, 227.

7. St. Augustine, "Sermon 57," 7, quoted in CCC, 2837.

8. Benedict XVI, "Homily for the Mass at the Twentieth World Youth Day, August 21, 2005," accessed June 2, 2014, http://www.vatican.va/holy_father/benedict_xvi/homilies/2005/documents/hf_ben-xvi_Hom_20050821_20th-world-youth-day_en.html.\

9. Equipped for the Day's Service

1. "The Concluding Rites," *Roman Missal*, 671–673.

2. Ibid.

3. Francis, *Evangelii Gaudium (The Joy of the Gospel)*, Encyclical Letter (Washington: United States Conference of Catholic Bishops, 2013), 120.

4. Paul VI, *Evangelii Nuntiandi (On Evangelization in the Modern World)*, Encyclical Letter (Boston: Pauline Books and Media, 1976), 21.

5. Ibid., 22.

Appendix I: Prayers before Mass

1. Adapted from "Prayer of St. Ambrose (Before Mass)," *Catholic Online,* accessed February 19, 2014, http://www.catholic.org/prayers/prayer.php?p=127.

2. St. Thomas Aquinas, "A Prayer before Mass," *EWTN: Global Catholic Network,* accessed February 19, 2014, https://www.ewtn.com/Devotionals/prayers/bmass.htm.

3. St. Thomas Aquinas, *Pange Lingua Gloriosi,* trans. E. Caswall, *EWTN: Global Catholic Network,* accessed February 19, 2013, https://www.ewtn.com/library/PRAYER/PANGE.TXT.

4. Adapted from the "*Te Deum,*" ancient hymn of the Church, accessed February 18, 2014, http://www.angelfire.com/md/Orastie/tedevers.html.

Appendix II: Prayers after Mass

1. The "*Anima Christi,*" the "Prayer of St. Thomas Aquinas," and the "Prayer of St. Bonaventure" are adapted from *Dominican Priests & Brothers of the Holy Face of Jesus,* accessed February 19, 2014, http://www.thirdorderofsaint-dominic.org/Prayers.htm.

2. "Prayer of St. Ignatius of Loyola," *EWTN: Global Catholic Network,* accessed February 19, 2014, https://www.ewtn.com/Devotionals/prayers/amass.htm.

3. St. Thomas Aquinas, "*Adoro Te Devote,*" accessed February 19, 2014, http://www.catholicculture.org/culture/liturgicalyear/activities/view.cfm?id=1083.

4. Adapted from http://www.angelfire.com/md/Orastie/tedevers.html, accessed February 18, 2014.

Appendix III: The General Roman Calendar Adapted for the United States of America

1. Adapted from the "General Roman Calendar," *Roman Missal,* 121–132.

A popular Catholic author and speaker, **Bert Ghezzi** has written twenty-six books, including *The Heart of Catholicism*, *Voices of the Saints*, *Mystics and Miracles*, and *Prayers to the Holy Spirit*. Hundreds of his articles have appeared in the religious press.

Ghezzi has been involved in religious education for more than forty years. He has served as a leader and teacher in several Catholic renewal movements and has spoken at numerous educational and renewal conferences throughout the United States and Canada. He appears frequently as a guest on EWTN, which also features his television series *Signs of Our Times*. Ghezzi is often interviewed on Catholic radio and his two-minute spots on saints play regularly on EWTN radio.

After receiving his doctorate from the University of Notre Dame, Ghezzi worked for seven years as a professor at Grand Valley State University in Michigan. He has served as a senior editor for five publishing companies since 1975 and now works as an acquisitions editor for Our Sunday Visitor's book division.

Bert and Mary Lou, his wife of fifty years, have seven children and sixteen grandchildren. They live in Winter Park, Florida.

Founded in 1865, Ave Maria Press,
a ministry of the Congregation of
Holy Cross, is a Catholic publishing
company that serves the spiritual and
formative needs of the Church and its
schools, institutions, and ministers;
Christian individuals and families; and
others seeking spiritual nourishment.

For a complete listing of titles from

Ave Maria Press

Sorin Books

Forest of Peace

Christian Classics

visit www.avemariapress.com

ave maria press® / Notre Dame, IN 46556
A Ministry of the United States Province of Holy Cross